Tabernacle Gifts

Our First Day in Heaven

Evangelical
First Edition, 2001

Michael Zarlengo

Copyright © 2001 Michael Zarlengo
All Rights Reserved under International Copyright Law.

ISBN 0-970454-81-3
Library of Congress Control Number: 00-093271

No portion of this book may be reproduced, stored in a retrieval system, or transmitted, in any form or by any means, electronic, mechanical, photocopy, recording, or other, without permission from the publisher.

Scripture quotations indicated NIV are taken from The HOLY BIBLE, NEW INTERNATIONAL VERSION®. NIV®. Copyright © 1973, 1978, 1984 by International Bible Society. Used by permission of Zondervan Publishing House and Hodder & Stoughton Limited. The "NIV" and "New International Version" trademarks are registered in the United States Patent and Trademark Office by International Bible Society. UK trademark number 1448790.

Scripture quotations indicated NASB are taken from The NEW AMERICAN STANDARD BIBLE®, © Copyright The Lockman Foundation 1960, 1962, 1963, 1968, 1971, 1972, 1973, 1975, 1977, 1995. Used by permission. (www.Lockman.org)

Scripture quotations indicated NKJV are taken from The New King James Version, copyright © 1979,1980,1982, Thomas Nelson, Inc., Publishers. Used by permission.

Scripture quotations indicated KJV are taken from The King James Version of the Bible.

Artwork: "Moses' Tabernacle in the Wilderness" © 1976 John E. Gilman

Publisher: Michael Zarlengo Publishing
17194 Preston Road Suite 123-142
Dallas, Texas 75248; SAN 253-4576

Printed in the United States of America

This book is dedicated to my wife of twenty-four years, Marcy. Without her encouragement, this work would not have been completed.

Acknowledgments

The author would like to acknowledge the efforts and insightful commentary toward this work by the following people:

Dr. Daniel L. Akin, Mike Buster, Pastor D. Samuel Dennis, Drew Dickens, Dean Fuller, Nawanda Fuller, Caroline Gilman, Don McMinn, David Zarlengo, Rev. Gary Zarlengo, Marcy Zarlengo, Rebecca Zarlengo, and Steven Zarlengo

Contents

Foreword: Dr. Daniel L. Akin	9
Chapter 1: The Picture	11
Chapter 2: The Tabernacle	15
Chapter 3: The Day of Atonement	25
Chapter 4: The True Picture	31
Chapter 5: The True Day of Atonement	39
Chapter 6: Our First Day in Heaven	55
Chapter 7: Be Encouraged!	91
Epilogue	97
Appendix A: Commentary on Leviticus 16	109
Appendix B: Traditional Interpretations & FAQs	121
Appendix C: Scripture Citations	137
Bibliography	139

Foreword

The Book of Hebrews teaches that Jesus is our great High Priest. Building on the imagery of the Old Testament sacrificial systems and the Day of Atonement, Hebrews affirms in the strongest terms the perfect sacrifice of Christ and His finished work as High Priest. Jesus Christ made propitiation for our sins (2:17), did away with sin (9:26), bore sin (9:28), and offered a perfect and final sacrifice for sin (10:12). Because of what Jesus did on the cross at Calvary, God remembers our sins no more (10:17). There is no longer a need for sacrifice for sin (10:18), and sin has been forgiven (10:18). The way of the Law and the levitical priestly system could not effectively deal with our sin (10:1–4, 6, 11). In contrast, the blood atonement of Jesus has dealt with sin once and for all (10:10–12). He has paved the way for free and bold access even into the Holy of Holies by His blood (10:10). Look at sin any way you will, Jesus has dealt with it.

Tabernacle Gifts

The work of Jesus is multifaceted. It would never be possible to exhaust its meaning and fathom its implications. In this work, *Tabernacle Gifts*, Michael Zarlengo gives attention to the tabernacle and Day of Atonement, and especially what the Book of Hebrews says concerning Christ's relationship to these important Old Testament realities. Michael explores possible understandings of Christ's work in heaven and present implications for the life of the believer. He has pursued his thesis diligently and with zeal. His goal is to challenge all believers to respond in faithful obedience to the glorified Christ, who rightly deserves our very best. This book will make you think, challenge you, and, I pray, inspire you to love and obey Jesus with greater fervency than ever before. That is Michael's desire, and I believe our Lord will reward his labors.

Dr. Daniel L. Akin
Dean, School of Theology
The Southern Baptist Theological Seminary

Chapter 1

⇨ The Picture ⇦

When you look at the picture of the tabernacle, what do you see? Do you see a tired old tent, the picture of antiquity? Perhaps you see symbols having spiritual meanings but having little application for our daily Christian life. You may see the animal sacrifice as a reminder of Jesus' sacrifice for our sins. If you are now saved, does this picture offer any help on how you can mature as a Christian? As Internet-age Christians, is this picture relevant to us today? In this book we will seek out the answers to those questions by using Scripture to assemble the true picture.

The Bible has over fifty[1] chapters describing the tabernacle. Fifty *chapters*, not verses! This topic must be very important to God. While in the desert,

---

[1] *The breakdown is: in Exodus, 13 chapters; in Leviticus, 18 chapters; in Numbers, 13 chapters; in Deuteronomy, 2 chapters; and in Hebrews, 4 chapters.*

Tabernacle Gifts

and for a time in Canaan, the children of Israel used the tabernacle as their place of worship; later, Solomon built a permanent place of worship by converting the tabernacle into the temple.[i] The Holy Spirit then wrote many more chapters about the temple.

Why is the tabernacle so important? To answer that and related questions, we'll separate our search into three parts. First, we'll observe what the tabernacle looked like and who worked there. Second, we'll describe how the tabernacle was used on the highest holy day of the year, the Day of Atonement. Finally, we'll determine the meanings and significance to us by using New Testament Scripture.

The tabernacle as well as the Day of Atonement have more than one meaning and more than one application. However, we will focus on those aspects that are most relevant to how we are to live as mature Christians today.

We will also see from New Testament Scripture that the tabernacle and the Day of Atonement clearly reveal to us what our first day in heaven will be like. We will gain a better understanding of how we can prepare for that incredible day.

Did Jesus bring God the Father gifts when He ascended to heaven? What type of reception was waiting for Him? We will answer those questions and see what the Bible teaches us regarding His spectacular gift-giving ceremony in heaven.

We work hard in this life to retire well. Yet earthly retirement lasts for a relatively short time. God's Word teaches Christians that our place and reward in

The Picture

heaven will depend on what we bring the Father. What does the Bible teach us we should do now, that will result in living well-rewarded in heaven? We know that our heavenly rest will last for an eternity.

Tabernacle Gifts

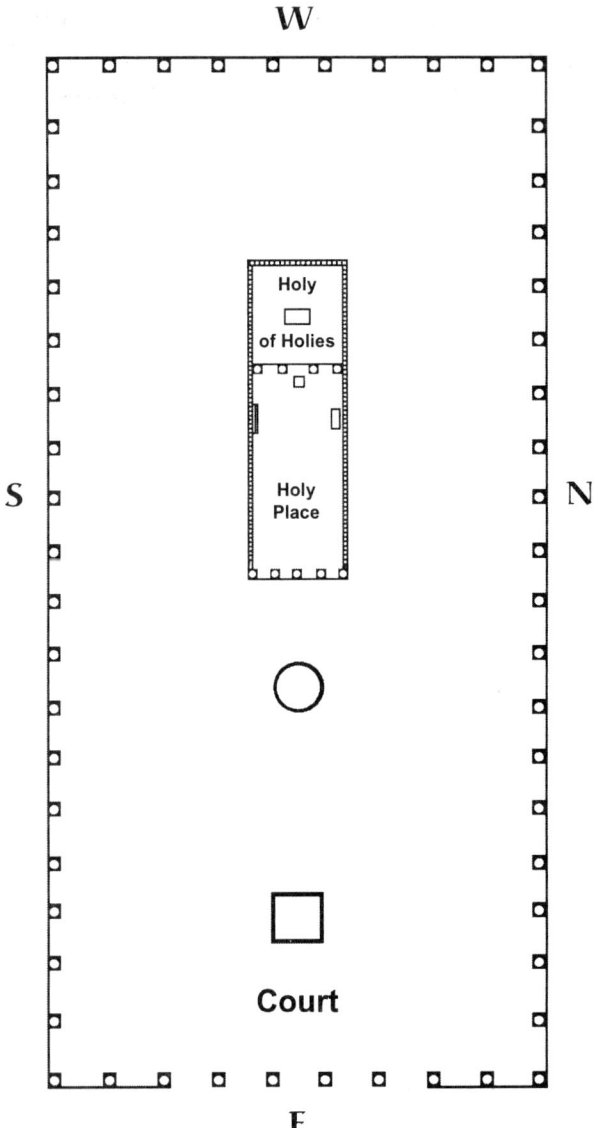

Chapter 2

~ The Tabernacle ~

First, we will examine the picture a little closer by briefly describing the tabernacle's structure, along with its seven primary pieces of furniture.

The tabernacle consisted of a tent with a courtyard (or court). The tent alone is sometimes referred to as the tabernacle. Why is the tent sometimes called the tabernacle if it refers only to the tent, not to the tent and courtyard? Perhaps you can think of it as a house with a porch. In order to walk into the house, you must first enter the porch. The porch is very much a part of the house, but technically it is not the house. For our purposes we will call the tent and court together the tabernacle, and the tent alone we will call the Tent of Meeting.

God required Moses to construct the tabernacle. God specified exactly how it was to look by showing Moses an image on Mount Sinai. Moses then instructed the artisans to make a copy of what he saw. It is

Tabernacle Gifts

important to note that the tabernacle Moses built was a copy.

Our fathers had the tabernacle of witness in the wilderness, as He appointed, instructing Moses to make it according to the pattern that he had seen, (Acts 7:44 NKJV)

The tabernacle was placed in the middle of the Israelite camp; it was surrounded by a white linen fence[ii] on all sides and had only one door, or gate, to enter. The gate was covered by a veil and located on the east side.[iii] The children of Israel were divided into twelve tribes and camped all around this structure.[iv] Three tribes camped on the north, three on the south, three to the west, and three to the east. Immediately around the tabernacle on all sides was the thirteenth[2] tribe, the Levites, who took care of the tabernacle. Moses and Aaron, both Levites, camped directly out from the east gate.[v]

---

[2]Jacob had twelve sons; each became the father of a tribe. In his culture the firstborn received a double inheritance over the other children. Jacob's firstborn was Reuben; however, Jacob took Reuben's birthright away from him because Reuben slept with Jacob's concubine, Bilhah. Jacob named Joseph as his firstborn instead and gave him a double portion of the land, his inheritance, by dividing Joseph's tribe into two tribes, Manasseh and Ephraim. These were Joseph's two sons. Hence we have thirteen tribes. It is also interesting to note that Jacob took away the birthright of Joseph's firstborn, Manasseh, and gave it to Ephraim, his brother. Later, in Psalm 78, God took away Ephraim's birthright and gave it to Judah. Jesus is out of the tribe of Judah.

The Tabernacle

⇜ The Inspection ⇝

Once the tabernacle was finished, Moses inspected it to determine if it was correctly built. Let's imagine walking with Moses through the tabernacle on his inspection. When Moses entered the court, he saw two items that formed a straight line from the east gate to the tent that was toward the back of the court. The first item was a large copper altar.[vi] This altar had fire under it with a grate over the fire. Animal sacrifices were to be burned on this altar. Walking around the altar, Moses came to a large copper basin full of water. This basin, called the laver, would be used as a place to wash after sacrificing. On the other side of the laver was the Tent of Meeting. Moses was to meet with God in this tent. Moses entered through its only door, which was on the east side of the tent. The door was covered with a veil.[vii]

The Tent of Meeting was divided into two chambers, separated by another veil. The first chamber, or outer room, was called the Holy Place. Once inside the Holy Place, Moses could see three pieces of furniture. On Moses' left (south side) was a golden candlestick (or lampstand) with oil lamps on seven branches,[viii] and on his right (north side[ix]) was a golden table with twelve loaves of unleavened bread. This bread was placed into two stacks of six, along with some pure incense. The bread was to be eaten every seven days, after which the stacks were to be renewed.[x]

Tabernacle Gifts

In front of Moses was a golden altar[xi] about three feet high. However, the location of this altar would change on the Day of Atonement. On that day, it was to be moved from the Holy Place to the other side of the veil and placed into the second chamber.[3]

Unlike the altar outside, this golden altar did not have fire under it. It would be used as a place to burn incense. The incense, along with coals, was to be put in a censer and placed on this altar. Directly behind the golden altar was a large veil. The veil was fifteen feet high and fifteen feet wide and four inches thick; it separated the second chamber of the Tent of Meeting from the first chamber.[xii] This second chamber, or inner room, was called the Holy of Holies or, in some translations, the Most Holy Place.

Sometimes the two rooms were referred to as the outer tabernacle and inner tabernacle. In order to walk into the Holy of Holies, it was necessary for Moses to go beyond the veil. Moses could not enter the veil through two parts like a drape, nor could he go around either side of the veil. The only way for him to walk from the Holy Place to the Holy of Holies was to go under the veil.

---

[3] Most Bible commentators believe the golden altar was not moved on the Day of Atonement. However, when the Day of Atonement is described in Leviticus 16, the incense is described as burned in the Holy of Holies (Lev. 16:12–13), which implies the golden altar was now there. Additionally, and most importantly, when the writer of Hebrews discusses the Day of Atonement (Heb. 9:4), he places the golden altar in the Holy of Holies. Regardless of placement, its meaning to us is not affected.

The Tabernacle

Once inside the Holy of Holies, Moses saw two items of furniture: a golden box called the Ark[xiii] and its solid gold lid, called the Mercy Seat.[xiv] The two together, lid and box, were called the Ark of the Covenant. The Ark contained three items: the tablets of stone with the Ten Commandments, Aaron's rod that budded, and a golden bowl of manna. The Mercy Seat had two golden angels on either side. It was from this Mercy Seat Throne that God would speak to Moses in an audible voice.[xv]

After his inspection, Moses approved the tabernacle's construction and dedicated it to God. Imagine Moses' joy at seeing that all the work was done according to God's requirement.[xvi]

⁀ The Light ⁀

Once the Glory of God filled the tabernacle,[xvii] Moses saw that three distinct lights lighted it. The only light inside the Holy Place was from the candlestick, which was kept continually lit.[xviii] The only light inside the Holy of Holies came from above the Mercy Seat Throne. This supernatural light fully lit the Holy of Holies and was the Glory of God.[xix] Above the tent stood a cloud pillar during the day, which became a pillar of fire at night.[xx] This pillar shaded the sunlight during the day (regulated the light) and lit the night sky. It was a constant reminder to the Israelites that God was with them. When this pillar moved, the

Tabernacle Gifts

children of Israel would break camp and follow it; when this pillar remained stationary, they would set up camp.[xxi]

The Materials

God had instructed Moses to use wood, copper,[4] and gold when constructing the tabernacle furniture. The laver was made of solid copper; the candlestick and Mercy Seat were made of solid gold. The remaining items were made of wood covered with copper or gold. Why wood covered with metal? The tabernacle was not permanent and was moved often. Using wood made it lighter and easier to move. In total there were seven items of furniture, the Ark and Mercy Seat counted separately. In addition, there were many accessory items made of copper and gold, such as censers, bowls, incense containers, oil containers, wick trimmers, and shovels, all used to support the primary items of furniture.

Later, when Solomon built the temple (which was a permanent structure) all the main pieces of furniture were either solid copper or solid gold. Solomon also placed more of the same items in the temple (such as ten candlesticks and ten lavers), along with having made other changes.

---

[4]*Some Bible translations consider the metal used to be bronze, not copper; however, "New Unger's Bible Dictionary" states that the metal was "most likely" copper.*

The Tabernacle

The Picture in Hebrews

The writer of Hebrews, who we will consider to be the apostle Paul, gives us a succinct portrait of the Tent of Meeting. Notice that Paul is describing the furniture arrangement for the Day of Atonement, as the golden altar is in the Holy of Holies.

For there was a tabernacle prepared, the outer one, in which were the lampstand and the table and the sacred bread; this is called the holy place. Behind the second veil there was a tabernacle which is called the Holy of Holies, having a golden altar of incense and the ark of the covenant covered on all sides with gold, in which was a golden jar holding the manna, and Aaron's rod which budded, and the tables of the covenant; and above it were the cherubim of glory overshadowing the mercy seat; but of these things we cannot now speak in detail. (Heb. 9:2–5 NASB)

The Priests

God not only showed Moses what the tabernacle should look like, but He also gave him instructions as to who should work there. The people who worked inside the tabernacle were the priests. There was one high priest and many assistant priests.[xxii] The high priest was an appointed position, and his term was

Tabernacle Gifts

for life. Moses appointed Aaron as the first high priest. The high priest was to represent the people to God. The high priests, as well as the assistant priests, were from the tribe of Levi. However, not all Levites were priests. The non-priest Levites could enter the tabernacle court and work with the altar and the laver, but they could not work in the Tent of Meeting. They were not even allowed to look inside.[xxiii]

The assistant priests could work in the court and enter the Tent of Meeting; however, they were only allowed to work in the Holy Place. They were not allowed to enter the Holy of Holies. In the court, they would offer sacrifices on the altar. In the Holy Place, they would light the candlestick, eat the bread every seven days and then replace (renew) it, and offer incense on the golden altar, along with other duties. The high priest alone could enter the Holy of Holies, and this occurred just once a year, on the Day of Atonement.[5]

There are many more details concerning the tabernacle's construction, its use, and the priests. However, this brief summary, like Paul's brief summary, will be sufficient for us to search out these matters.

It is the glory of God to conceal a matter; to search out a matter is the glory of kings. (Prov. 25:2 NIV)

---

[5]*The high priest did have to enter the Holy of Holies on other occasions, such as when he had to pack the items to move camp. However, this is the only day of the year that he entered the Holy of Holies to conduct a special observance.*

Woodcut 1861, Andreas Muller: High Priest with assistant priest and non-priest Levite.

Chapter 3

⇁ The Day of Atonement ⇀

Now that the tabernacle picture has been described and we know who worked there, let's look at what took place on the day God told Moses was the most important and holiest day of the year, the Day of Atonement.[xxiv] The Day of Atonement is described in Leviticus 16. It was celebrated as the one day each year that atonement (or purification) was made for all the sins of the children of Israel.[xxv] In the Hebrew calendar, this day was celebrated on the tenth day of the seventh month. This day is still celebrated by Jews today during the fall and is called Yom Kippur.

Perhaps we can visualize Aaron, the first high priest, reverently performing this ceremony. In the days just prior to the Day of Atonement, the high priest would separate himself, to some extent, from

Tabernacle Gifts

the people. He would prepare himself for this very holy event. On that day, he wore a simple white robe, not his usual ornate high priest robe. He walked through the east gate into the court, leading a large bull in one hand and a ram (male sheep) in the other. The bull was his first sacrifice for the altar. The ram was set to the side, to be sacrificed later in the day.

    He slaughtered the bull and burned it on the altar. He only burned the best parts of the bull: the head, internal organs, and fat. He did not burn the hide and hoofs, but instead placed them aside in a pile. These items were considered the rejected parts. The fire burned brightly due to the large size and the abundant fat of the bull. Once this was completed, he placed some of the blood in a bowl, gathered up two handfuls of incense, and placed it in a censer. Then he walked toward the laver. After washing at the laver, he entered the Tent of Meeting.

    He walked through the veil door into the Holy Place and proceeded to the next veil. Then he stooped down and went under this veil into the Holy of Holies. He was now before the very presence of God. He paused and burned incense in the censer on the golden altar. The smoke filled the Holy of Holies. He then walked around the altar and stood before the Ark and Mercy Seat. There he sprinkled the bull's blood on the front of the Mercy Seat seven times. Scripture says he sprinkled the blood eastward (down) and before (across) the front.[xxvi] Think of the fingers of one hand dipped in the blood, the arm raised, and then in a downward motion waved

The Day of Atonement

toward the Mercy Seat ending at his side (traveling east) and then waved across the middle. It is interesting to note that this movement would have made the sign of a cross, seven times.

Meanwhile, one of the assistant priests gathered up the parts of the bull that had been rejected and took them out through the east gate. He walked right through the camp, passing thousands of Israelites who were witnessing these events. Once outside the camp, he made a pile of wood and burned the discarded remains.

The high priest returned to the tabernacle court, where assistant priests brought him two goats and a ram. This ram was also set to the side, to be sacrificed later in the day. The high priest threw a type of dice, called lots, over the goats. The high priest let the lots decide which goat would be sacrificed.[xxvii]

The sacrificial goat was led to the altar and slaughtered. The high priest took the best parts of the goat and burned them. He set aside the parts that were considered rejected as he had done with the bull. The fire would burn brightly, but not nearly so brightly as the bull's; the goat was much smaller and had less fat. The high priest then placed some of the goat's blood in a bowl. He proceeded to the laver and washed again, but this time he did not bring any incense with him. He then entered the Tent of Meeting. Once there, he went under the veil and sprinkled the goat's blood on the front of the Mercy Seat Throne in the sign of a cross, seven times, just as he had done with the bull's blood.

Tabernacle Gifts

Again, an assistant priest gathered up the rejected parts of the goat and followed the same route taken by the priest who had earlier discarded the rejected parts of the bull. He followed the exact path, passing thousands of people. He then placed the discarded parts of the goat on the same wood pile as the bull's and burned them.[6]

At this point, the high priest came into the court and took hold of the other goat. He laid his hands on it, confessed the people's sins, and then brought the goat back to the east gate. Arriving at the east gate, he chose an available man (not a priest) to walk the goat outside the camp. This man would take a different route than the two priests who had taken the rejected parts. Once outside the camp he would simply let the goat wander into the wilderness. This goat was called the scapegoat.

With his work nearly complete, the high priest turned his attention to the two rams. He slaughtered them and burned the entire portion of each ram (no rejected parts), at the same time, on the altar. He also added some of the fat that he had held back from the bull and goat sacrifices.

---

[6]*It is also possible that both the bull and goat remains were taken outside the camp together toward the end of the ceremony. However, it is more consistent with sacrificial practices for this to be removed as they proceeded during the day. Regardless of timing, the meaning to us is not affected.*

[7]*There were other activities that occurred on this day; however, the primary sacrifices and activities described above are sufficient for us to consider in this book.*

The Day of Atonement

The Day of Atonement was finished. The high priest then washed, put on his ornate robe (by now his white robe was stained with blood), and rejoined the people. The multitude of the children of Israel looked expectantly for the high priest to come out of the tabernacle. When he reemerged, he blessed the people and told them that God had accepted the sacrifices.[7] Atonement had been made. The people were very pleased. God was very pleased.

Chapter 4

～ The True Picture ～

Although the tabernacle, the priests, and the Day of Atonement were present on the earth, all three were symbolic of a much greater spiritual reality. Restated a different way, God designed the tabernacle and the Day of Atonement ceremony as an annual living picture of an event that was to take place in heaven with heavenly participants. The true tabernacle is heaven; the one created on earth was a mere copy of heaven. Jesus is the true High Priest, who, on a certain day, entered heaven and went into its Tent of Meeting to conduct heaven's holiest ceremony, the true Day of Atonement.

～ The True Tabernacle ～

The true tabernacle is heaven; the one on the earth was a copy of heaven.

Tabernacle Gifts

When Christ came as high priest of the good things that are already here, he went through the greater and more perfect tabernacle that is not man-made, that is to say, not a part of this creation. (Heb. 9:11 NIV)

For Christ did not enter a holy place made with hands, a mere copy of the true one, but into heaven itself, now to appear in the presence of God for us; (Heb. 9:24 NASB)

Jesus Is the True High Priest

Ever since creating mankind, God desired fellowship with mankind, but mankind sinned and became separated from God. God then created a covenant with mankind called the Mosaic covenant (also called the Law). Mankind could not meet the terms of the Law, and as a result earned the penalty, which is eternal separation from God.[lvi] Therefore, God desired to make a new covenant with us to restore fellowship. He appointed His Son, Jesus, to be the mediator of this new covenant. Jesus was the only one who could fulfill this unique role because He is God who became man.[lvii] While on earth He remained God; however, He voluntarily did not use or exercise certain attributes of His Glory.[lviii] That is why we say there is no one like Jesus. There is no one like Jesus! Since

The True Picture

Jesus is a mediator between God and mankind, His role and title is High Priest.

**Seeing then that we have a great High Priest who has passed through the heavens, Jesus the Son of God, let us hold fast our confession.
(Heb. 4:14 NKJV)**

The office of high priest was an appointed position. Jesus was appointed by God to be the High Priest of the new covenant just as Aaron was appointed by Moses to be the high priest of the old covenant. Jesus, like the earthly high priests, was also appointed for life, but unlike those high priests His life never ends. Because this was a new covenant, it was fitting that Jesus be out of a new tribe, not from the priest tribe of Levi, but a different tribe, to emphasize the new covenant. That different tribe was Judah.[xxviii] The tribe of Judah was camped on the east side of the tabernacle, right out from the east gate, or door, just beyond Moses' and Aaron's tents.

Jesus was also different from the earthly high priests because he was a Royal High Priest. He is royalty because He is the Son of a King, God Almighty. The only example in the Bible of both a king and priest prior to Jesus is Melchizedek. That is why Jesus is called a priest in the order of Melchizedek.[c]

No one takes this honor upon himself; he must be called by God, just as Aaron was. So Christ also did not take upon himself the glory of

Tabernacle Gifts

becoming a high priest. But God said to him, "You are my Son; today I have become your Father." And he says in another place, "You are a priest forever, in the order of Melchizedek." (Heb. 5:4–6 NIV)

Now there have been many of those priests, since death prevented them from continuing in office; but because Jesus lives forever, he has a permanent priesthood. (Heb. 7:23–24 NIV)

As appointed High Priest, Jesus was to represent mankind and reconcile us to God. In order to do that He had to become a man. He had to be like us in every way and pay our penalty for breaking the first covenant. He also had to suffer temptation like us but remain sinless, so that He could meet all the terms of the first covenant and mediate the new one.

For this reason he had to be made like his brothers in every way, in order that he might become a merciful and faithful high priest in service to God, and that he might make atonement for the sins of the people. Because he himself suffered when he was tempted, he is able to help those who are being tempted. (Heb. 2:17–18 NIV)

Our High Priest, Jesus, who was appointed by God and who represented us before God, lived a perfect life. He then sacrificed Himself and paid the penalty for our sin, thus restoring permanent fellow-

The True Picture

ship with God. God showed His approval of the High Priest's sacrifice by raising Jesus from the dead.[lix] The new covenant allows people to accept the work of Jesus and accept the fact that God approved His work. Under this new covenant God will remember their sins no more.[lx]

⁓ The True Assistants ⁓

The assistant priests are analogous in certain respects to obedient[lxi] Christians today. Just as the Old Testament assistant priests were considered under Aaron's order of priesthood, Christians are now priests under the new order of our High Priest, Jesus. Our order is the new king and priest order, started by Jesus.[8] It can be said of us, "We are priests forever in the order of Jesus." What a privilege!

But you are a chosen people, a royal priesthood, a holy nation, a people belonging to God, that you may declare the praises of him who called you out of darkness into his wonderful light. (1 Pet. 2:9 NIV)

And have made us kings and priests to our God; And we shall reign on the earth." (Rev. 5:10 NKJV)

---

[8]*That is one reason why the least in the kingdom of heaven are said to be greater (in honor) than John the Baptist. Our designation as kings and priests is a greater honor because we came after the finished work of the great High Priest: Jesus' life, death, and resurrection.*

Tabernacle Gifts

To summarize, the true tabernacle is actually heaven and the one on earth was simply a copy. Jesus is our Royal High Priest and Christians[lxii] are Christ's royal assistant priests.

≈ The True Day of ≈ Atonement

We learn from Paul's description below that our High Priest, Jesus, performed the Day of Atonement ceremony on the day He entered heaven. Christ entered God's Tent of Meeting in heaven and went into the Holy of Holies with His own blood to represent us. He only had to do that once, unlike the earthly high priests who had to repeat the Day of Atonement ceremony annually, in the tabernacle copy, with a bull's blood.

For Christ did not enter a man-made sanctuary that was only a copy of the true one; he entered heaven itself, now to appear for us in God's presence. Nor did he enter heaven to offer himself again and again, the way the high priest enters the Most Holy Place every year with blood that is not his own. (Heb. 9:24–25 NIV)

≈ More Truth ≈

The bull symbolized Jesus' sacrifices and the sacrifice of His human body.

The True Picture

By this will we have been sanctified through the offering of the body of Jesus Christ once for all. (Heb. 10:10 NASB)

    We will look more into Jesus' sacrifices, as well as the meaning of the goats and rams in later chapters. We will also seek to better understand our role as assistant priests and our role as kings. In addition, we'll search out other related matters and details, regarding each of these truths.

    We need to pause and reflect on this great Mediator, who became like us in order to restore us to God. How He must love the Father and how He must love us to give up so much and suffer so much to mediate this covenant. In order to obtain the benefits of this new covenant, we accepted the work of the true High Priest, believing that God approved His work. When we accepted the Royal High Priest, we accepted His work. If you do not know this great Mediator and Royal High Priest, now is the time. If you confess Him with your mouth as your High Priest and Lord and believe in your heart that God raised Him from the dead, Jesus' work will save you, and all your sins will be permanently forgotten![xxix]

"**FOR I WILL BE MERCIFUL TO THEIR INIQUITIES, AND I WILL REMEMBER THEIR SINS NO MORE.**" **(Heb. 8:12 NASB)**

Chapter 5

~ The True Day of ~ Atonement

In this chapter we will look at one of the most exciting and spectacular events ever recorded in God's Word. This event occurred in heaven following the perfect work of Jesus on the cross. It is considered God's most important and holiest ceremony. When did our Royal High Priest walk through the true tabernacle and conduct the true Day of Atonement ceremony? The following scriptures tell us about this dramatic event. We will attempt to fill in the picture, realizing that all of the details have not been revealed. This great ceremony took place when Jesus left earth and entered heaven after His resurrection, two thousand years ago.

After his suffering, he showed himself to these men and gave many convincing proofs that he

Tabernacle Gifts

was alive. He appeared to them over a period of forty days and spoke about the kingdom of God. (Acts 1:3 NIV)

After he said this, he was taken up before their very eyes, and a cloud hid him from their sight. (Acts 1:9 NIV)

What we do on earth is revealed in heaven.[lxiii] Jesus fully atoned for our sin on the cross. When He returned to heaven His atonement work on earth was revealed and, according to the Book of Hebrews, applied as He walked through the true tabernacle to conduct the Day of Atonement ceremony.

How can we know what Jesus did in heaven? The old covenant had regulations for the Day of Atonement ceremony, and it also had an earthly tabernacle.

Now the first covenant had regulations for worship and also an earthly sanctuary. (Heb. 9:1 NIV)

However, both the earthly tabernacle *and* the earthly regulations were copies. Christ, the mediator of the new covenant, went through[lxiv] the true tabernacle. The true High Priest encountered in the heavenly tabernacle the same items copied in the earthly tabernacle. He would also have fulfilled the true regulations with His better work.[lxv] It is informative for our search to examine the *pattern* of regulations that were followed.

The True Day of Atonement

It was necessary, then, for the copies of heavenly things to be purified with these sacrifices, but the heavenly things themselves with better sacrifices than these. (Heb. 9:23 NIV)

    Jesus had completed His new covenant work on earth. He had become like us, had lived a perfect life, and had died to restore fellowship between God and mankind. Atonement had been made. God had raised Him from the dead, and for forty days Jesus showed Himself to the disciples.

    There is mystery[lxvi] surrounding our Lord's activity during the days leading up to His ascension. No scholar of Scripture denies this. Hebrews informs us of His entrance into the Holy of Holies in heaven with His blood atonement. While we cannot be certain, perhaps this explains, in part, the separateness Jesus kept to some degree from His people during this time. It follows what the earthly high priest did before the Hebrew Day of Atonement.

Jesus said, "Do not hold on to me, for I have not yet returned to the Father. Go instead to my brothers and tell them, 'I am returning to my Father and your Father, to my God and your God.'"(John 20:17 NIV)

    Once Jesus ascended into heaven, it is believed He entered through heaven's east gate.[9] He wore a simple white robe stained with blood[lxvii] and walked

Tabernacle Gifts

right before God's altar. He did not have to bring a bull with Him; the sacrifice He brought was Himself. There the fire was burning greatly representing His great atonement sacrifice on the cross.[lxviii] This is God's altar and fire where Jesus' and the Christian's work was and will be revealed.

Therefore, since we receive a kingdom which cannot be shaken, let us show gratitude, by which we may offer to God an acceptable service with reverence and awe; for our God is a consuming fire. (Heb. 12:28–29 NASB)

Jesus then took His own blood and two handfuls of incense[lxxxiii] in a censer and walked toward the laver.

He did not enter by means of the blood of goats and calves; but he entered the Most Holy Place once for all by his own blood, having obtained eternal redemption. (Heb. 9:12 NIV)

At the laver He may have washed, perhaps representing His obedient baptism and the water of God's Word with which he spoke to men and cleansed men's evil consciences while on earth.[lxxix]

---

[9]"*And the glory of the Lord came into the house [Heb. 3:1–6] by way of the gate facing toward the east" (Ezek. 43:4 NASB). A surprising event occurred at this gate when Jesus approached it; see the epilogue for a description of that event.*

The True Day of Atonement

"You are already clean because of the word which I have spoken to you. (John 15:3 NASB)

so that He might sanctify her [the church], having cleansed her by the washing of water with the word, (Eph. 5:26 NASB)

Then Jesus entered into heaven's Tent of Meeting. There on His left was the golden candlestick, which represents the church He had established on earth.[xxx] The base or foundation of the candlestick many believe represents Christ. This candlestick was burning with oil. Oil often represents the Holy Spirit, that Spirit who led Christ on earth and returned Him to heaven.[xxxi] The light represents the light of God's Word, with which He reveals the way. On the right (north side[10]) was the golden table. Some believe this represents His millennial kingdom on earth that He will someday rule. On the table were the twelve loaves of unleavened bread, which represent that His kingdom is made up of cleansed people (no leaven or yeast, which represents sin). The twelve loaves represent that His people will be divided[11] into the twelve tribes of Israel,[lxix] over whom the apostles will rule in that kingdom.

---

[10] *North is representative of the kingdom's location, "Beautiful for situation, the joy of the whole earth, is mount Zion, on the sides of the north, the city of the great King" (Ps. 48:2 KJV). Jesus' millennial kingdom will be ruled from Jerusalem.*

[11] *Gentile believers are considered a part of (grafted to) the tribe of Levi (Heb. 2:11), "the priest tribe," and like the Old Testament assistant priests will be placed throughout all the tribes in His kingdom.*

Tabernacle Gifts

and just as My Father has granted Me a kingdom, I grant you [the apostles] that you may eat and drink at My table in My kingdom, and you will sit on thrones judging the twelve tribes of Israel. (Luke 22:29–30 NASB)

Next, Jesus stood in the place where the veil in the earthly tabernacle had stood. Remember that this veil had blocked the way to the Holy of Holies. The veil represented His flesh.

by a new and living way which He inaugurated for us through the veil, that is, His flesh, (Heb. 10:20 NASB)

The veil in heaven was no longer there. On earth it was torn from top to bottom when Jesus died[xxxii]; however, in heaven it was completely removed.[12] Why did the veil, which separated God from the sight of the earthly assistant priests, represent Jesus' flesh? God is Holy; He cannot have before Him anyone who is not perfect. Jesus, in the flesh, led a perfect life.

---

[12]*His body was taken down from the cross. The Father resurrected Him and He lives as our Divine God (Heb. 5:8–9).*
[13]*Sheol is where the Old Testament righteous and wicked waited, separated by a chasm. When the Old Testament righteous were taken to heaven, only the wicked remained there. Therefore, we now call this place hell, which continues to fill with those who are not saved when they die. It is also referred to as "under the earth" (Isa. 44:23, Ezek. 26:20). Later the contents of hell will be thrown into the lake of fire (Rev. 20:14–15). Also see Acts 2:27 where the apostle Peter quotes verse 10 of Psalm 16.*

The True Day of Atonement

Hence, the veil represented Jesus' flesh. Had Jesus not sacrificed that perfect life, the veil would still be up. Jesus laid down His life for us and through the death of His flesh He makes us holy; He made a way for us through the veil. Hallelujah!

The earthly high priest would stoop and go under the veil, which perhaps symbolized Jesus' death and that Jesus had descended to the lower, earthly regions.[lxx]

(What does "he ascended" mean except that he also descended to the lower, earthly regions? He who descended is the very one who ascended higher than all the heavens, in order to fill the whole universe.) (Eph. 4:9–10 NIV)

~ Sheol ~

Where did Jesus go when He descended, and when did this happen? The Old Testament righteous and wicked were in Sheol.[13] During Jesus' three days in the tomb, He went to Sheol and preached the truth to them.

For You will not abandon my soul to Sheol; Nor will You allow Your Holy One to undergo decay. (Ps. 16:10 NASB)

by whom also He went and preached to the spirits in prison, (1 Pet. 3:19 NKJV)

Tabernacle Gifts

Forty days later, He gathered the righteous and returned with them to the Father's tabernacle. That is why it is said, Jesus took captivity captive. He retrieved the Old Testament righteous from Sheol and brought them to heaven with Him.

Therefore He says: "When He ascended on high, He led captivity captive, And gave gifts to men." (Eph. 4:8 NKJV)

What was Sheol like? Jesus, in Luke 16:19–31, gave a very detailed description of it. Sheol was where the Old Testament righteous and Old Testament wicked waited, separated by a great chasm.

And besides all this, between us and you a great chasm has been fixed, so that those who want to go from here to you cannot, nor can anyone cross over from there to us.' (Luke 16:26 NIV)

Our true High Priest brought the Old Testament righteous with Him when He entered heaven. The first ram, which was walked into the court by the high priest on the Hebrew Day of Atonement, represented this, as the first half of the results of Christ's work: the Old Testament righteous. When this procession reached heaven's east gate, the angel guards initially hesitated to let them in![lxxi] This surprising event is described in detail in the epilogue of this book.

The True Day of Atonement

No one who is not made perfect and holy can come before God, not even the great Old Testament righteous men and women.[lxxii] They (like the children of Israel) waited outside of heaven's Tent of Meeting while the great High Priest went in.[lxxiii] They were allowed access through the east gate because at this point they had accepted Jesus as their Lord and personal Savior and witnessed that God had raised Him from the dead.[14]

◦ Holy of Holies ◦

Returning to Jesus' walk...He saw the Father in heaven to whom He had gone back after thirty-three years on the earth.

I came from the Father and entered the world; now I am leaving the world and going back to the Father." (John 16:28 NIV)

Jesus approached the golden altar, which represented His worship, praise, and prayers to the Father while on earth.[15]

---

[14]*This was true for all the Old Testament righteous right up to the thief who was hung on the cross beside Jesus. The thief asked Jesus to remember him when He entered His Kingdom. Jesus told the thief that **today** they would be together in paradise (Luke 23:43). However, **3 days later** Jesus told Mary Magdalene that He had not yet been to the Father (John 20:17). This is because the paradise Jesus was referring to was the righteous side of Sheol. Later the thief (now a Christian) joined the procession to heaven.*

Tabernacle Gifts

During the days of Jesus' life on earth, he offered up prayers and petitions with loud cries and tears to the one who could save him from death, and he was heard because of his reverent submission. (Heb. 5:7 NIV)

In front of the golden altar, Jesus paused and burned the incense. Smoke filled the Holy of Holies. The incense represents His perfect work. The fragrance of it was acceptable to God. Symbolically, the two handfuls indicated that He had completed the full requirement of His work[lxxx]; He could gather up no more. He led a perfect life in every respect. He was tempted in every way like us but remained sinless. His work was complete. The Ark itself represents Jesus. The three items in the box each represent an aspect of Jesus. The stone tablets with the Ten Commandments represent Jesus' perfect life; He fulfilled the Law, the old covenant. Aaron's rod that budded represents that Jesus was appointed by God as High Priest of the new covenant. Others had challenged Aaron as high priest, but the rod proved he was God's choice.[16] The manna represents Jesus as the new covenant. Manna gave life to the Israelites in the desert; Jesus, our Manna, gives us eternal life.

---

[15]*Jesus, along with the Holy Spirit, is coequal with the Father. Jesus' role as High Priest lasts forever; as High Priest, Jesus intercedes to the Father on our behalf (Heb. 7:24–25). The Trinity is a mystery.*

The True Day of Atonement

I am the living bread [Manna] that came down from heaven. If anyone eats of this bread, he will live forever. This bread is my flesh, which I will give for the life of the world." (John 6:51 NIV)

God the Father, to whom Jesus returned, was seated[lxxiv] on the solid gold Mercy Seat Throne.[lxxv] Finally, before the Throne of God, Jesus sprinkled His own blood seven times in the sign of His cross.[lxxvi]

and to Jesus, the mediator of a new covenant, and to the sprinkled blood, which speaks better than the blood of Abel. (Heb. 12:24 NASB)

All high priests were required to bring sacrificial gifts when they went before the Mercy Seat Throne on the Day of Atonement. The high priests were required to sprinkle the blood seven times. Jesus brought His Father seven sacrificial gifts gleaned from Philippians.[lxxxi] Seven, when used in the Bible, is God's number for spiritual perfection.

who, although He existed in the form of God, did not regard equality with God a thing to be grasped, but emptied Himself, taking the form of a bond-servant, and being made in the likeness

---

[16]*In Numbers 17 we are told that the children of Israel challenged Moses regarding Aaron's appointment as high priest. They felt that other people they chose could also serve God as high priest. Each tribe provided Moses with a rod to determine whom God appointed, and only Aaron's rod budded.*

Tabernacle Gifts

of men. Being found in appearance as a man, He humbled Himself by becoming obedient to the point of death, even death on a cross. (Phil. 2:6–8 NASB)

- who, although He existed in the form of God, did not regard equality with God a thing to be grasped,
- but emptied Himself,
- taking the form of a bond-servant,
- and being made in the likeness of men.
- Being found in the appearance as a man,
- He humbled Himself
- by becoming obedient to the point of death, even death on the cross.

Jesus' seven sacrifices made possible fellowship between God and mankind. The Father accepted Jesus' sacrifices.

At this point, three things happened. First, Jesus did something no earthly high priest ever did. He sat down! He sat on the right side of the Mercy Seat Throne where He shares it still with the Father. Where else could He sit? There was no other seat in the tabernacle! Sitting down is not only a physical act, it also represents His ruling authority as Majesty. For example, we say that an earthly monarch sits on the throne of a country, meaning that this person reigns. Jesus, along with the Father, reigns on the Throne of all creation!

The True Day of Atonement

Now the main point in what has been said is this: we have such a high priest, who has taken His seat at the right hand of the throne of the Majesty in the heavens, a minister in the sanctuary and in the true tabernacle, which the Lord pitched, not man. For every high priest is appointed to offer both gifts and sacrifices; so it is necessary that this high priest also have something to offer. (Heb. 8:1–3 NASB)

Second, on this day, God the Father rewarded Jesus for His seven sacrifices with seven exaltations. The following verses are also from Philippians and follow the verses recorded above.

For this reason also, God highly exalted Him, and bestowed on Him the name which is above every name, so that at the name of Jesus EVERY KNEE WILL BOW, of those who are in heaven and on earth and under the earth, and that every tongue will confess that Jesus Christ is Lord, to the glory of God the Father. (Phil. 2:9–11 NASB)

- For this reason also, God highly exalted Him,
- and bestowed on Him the name which is above every name,
- so that at the name of Jesus EVERY KNEE WILL BOW,
- of those who are in heaven

Tabernacle Gifts

- and on earth
- and under the earth,
- and that every tongue will confess that Jesus Christ is Lord, to the glory of God the Father.

    Each exaltation corresponds to each of Jesus' sacrificial gifts: While on earth He did not use or exercise certain attributes of His Glory; for this reason all attributes of His Glory were fully exalted. While on earth He gave up the independent use of His Divine attributes; for this reason now all are put under His direct authority and power. While on earth He took on our debt as the Father's servant; for this reason all will be His servants. While on earth He gave up His heavenly appearance; for this reason all those in heaven are His subjects. While on earth He lived like a man; for this reason all those on the earth will be His subjects. While on earth He humbled Himself by learning from His suffering; for this reason all those under the earth (His enemies) will be humbled. While on earth He was treated as a man and allowed Himself to be put to death on the cross; for this reason all will treat Him as Lord.

    Jesus received seven exaltations because of His seven sacrificial gifts. The scene described in chapter 5 of Revelation is an example of His highly exalted position. In this scene, God the Father had a scroll with seven seals that no one could open. A search was made in heaven, earth, and below the earth, but no one was found worthy (exalted) to open it. The

The True Day of Atonement

apostle John wept bitterly because of this. John was then comforted, because Jesus was found worthy to open the scroll. He was the only one worthy to break the seven seals because He was given seven exaltations, which He received as a result of His seven sacrifices. There is no one like Jesus!

And they sang a new song: "You are worthy to take the scroll and to open its [seven] seals, because you were slain, and with your blood you purchased men for God from every tribe and language and people and nation. (Rev. 5:9 NIV)

Finally, Jesus came out of heaven's Tent of Meeting and blessed the multitude of Old Testament righteous waiting for Him to bring His gifts before the Father. When He reemerged from the Tent of Meeting in all His Glory[17] and blessed them, we can be sure, there was a shout of joy the likes of which had never been heard. They would now be able to enter the Holy of Holies and enjoy eternal fellowship with God just as we will when we enter heaven.

These were all commended for their faith, yet none of them received what had been promised. God had planned something better for us so that only together with us would they be made perfect. (Heb. 11:39–40 NIV)

---

[17]*Represented by the high priest putting on his ornate robe.*

Tabernacle Gifts

Jesus' Day of Atonement ceremony was finished. What a glorious celebration!

Take another look at the tabernacle picture; do you see anything different? Do you see a Father waiting for a Son, a Father who had arranged the furniture to be representative of His Son? Do you see a Son who did not return to His Father empty-handed, and a Father who accepted His Son's gifts?

Just ten days later, God sent the Holy Spirit to earth to begin His work, on the Day of Pentecost.

Chapter 6

～ Our First Day in Heaven ～

The tabernacle and Day of Atonement ceremony also provide a description of a Christian's entry into heaven. They reveal what we can expect our first day in heaven. The sacrificial goat represented the sacrificial gifts of obedient Christians (Christ's assistant priests), which are brought by us to God. The second ram represented the second half of the results of Christ's work, the New Testament Christians.[18] In this chapter we will infer from Scripture what our walk will resemble when we go before God for the very first time.

When we die,[19] each of us will be called before the Throne of God and Christ, where our works will be accounted for and we will be rewarded.

---

[18]The assistant priests who brought the goats and ram to the high priest on the Hebrew Day of Atonement were portraying New Testament Christians bringing gifts to be tested by God's fire.[lxxxviii]

[19]Many Christians will be raptured rather then die. Raptured (con.)

Tabernacle Gifts

For we must all appear before the judgment seat of Christ, that each one may receive what is due him for the things done while in the body, whether good or bad [the not-good part of our works]. (2 Cor. 5:10 NIV)

Will there still be a Tent of Meeting to walk through when we arrive? The following scripture is from the second-to-last chapter of the Bible.

And I heard a loud voice from the throne, saying, "Behold, the tabernacle of God is among men, and He will dwell among them, and they shall be His people, and God Himself will be among them, (Rev. 21:3 NASB)

As goat's blood followed bull's blood, Christians will follow Christ's walk to God's Throne with their gifts. We will enter through heaven's east gate wearing white robes. As kings and priests, we will follow the path our Royal High Priest took into God's heav-

---

19(continued)Christians will all enter heaven at the same time, yet each will still be judged and rewarded individually (1Thess. 4:13–18). Also, some Bible commentators dispute the timing of our gift giving. They believe that this will occur not as we enter heaven but after all Christians have arrived in heaven (1Cor. 4:1–5). It is believed that the timing referred to in 1 Corinthians 4 is for raptured Christians, and regarding those who die, the Scripture states that once we leave this life we will be brought present before the Lord immediately: "We are confident, yes, well pleased rather to be absent from the body and to be present with the Lord" (2 Cor. 5:8 NKJV). Regardless of timing, the meaning to us is not affected.

Our First Day in Heaven

enly Tent of Meeting. Jesus is our forerunner. We will not stop just in the Holy Place; we will enter into the formerly veiled Holy of Holies, where Jesus went, and stand before God.

This hope we have as an anchor of the soul, a hope both sure and steadfast and one, which enters within the veil, where Jesus has entered as a forerunner for us, having become a high priest forever according to the order of Melchizedek. (Heb. 6:19–20 NASB)

～ We Enter Heaven ～

We are only allowed to enter through heaven's gate because we accepted Jesus as our Lord and personal Savior. At the moment of our salvation we became worthy to receive a robe, white and clean. We will be given a robe of fine white linen when we arrive. This represents our: salvation, cleansing from sin, and righteous acts.[xxxiii] (After salvation we are not to sin, and when we fail we are to confess our sin.[xxxi])

    We will come first in front of God's altar, where our Christian life on earth will be revealed. Our fire will burn brightly according to our service in this life, for we are called to lead a sacrificial life for Christ in order to bring God the Father gifts. However, just as a goat is small and lean in comparison to a bull, our sacrifice compared to Christ's will burn far less brightly than His.

Tabernacle Gifts

Therefore I urge you, brethren, by the mercies of God, to present your bodies a living and holy sacrifice, acceptable to God, which is your spiritual service of worship. (Rom. 12:1 NASB)

you also, as living stones, are being built up a spiritual house, a holy priesthood, to offer up spiritual sacrifices acceptable to God through Jesus Christ. (1 Pet. 2:5 NKJV)

The fire will reveal our earthly life's sacrificial gifts for God. We will gather up our gifts remaining after the fire tests them.

⁕ A Few Answers ⁕

Before we continue to examine our walk, let's clear up a few questions. When we studied earlier about the Day of Atonement, it was noticeable that the high priest was the primary one working, not the assistant priests. However, as observed, the assistant priests also had duties that day. Why are Christians now represented in the Day of Atonement? It is by Jesus alone, the true High Priest over the house of God, that we are able to enter the true tabernacle. The high priest working alone was to emphasize that we are allowed to present our life's work to God and to be in His house only due to the work, authority, and presence of Jesus.

Our First Day in Heaven

Therefore, brethren, having boldness to enter the Holiest by the blood of Jesus, by a new and living way which He consecrated for us, through the veil, that is, His flesh, and having a High Priest over the house of God, (Heb. 10:19–21 NKJV)

The high priest brought goat's blood before the Mercy Seat. How does this represent a Christian's gifts? Is this our blood? Gifts come from a true (sincere) heart. Jesus' blood is sprinkled on our hearts at the moment of salvation. Hence, this blood is still representative of Jesus' blood, but now it is over our hearts. Our sprinkled, true hearts produce gifts in this life, which are later brought to God.

let us draw near with a true heart in full assurance of faith, having our hearts sprinkled from an evil conscience and our bodies washed with pure water. (Heb. 10:22 NKJV)

To summarize, when we were saved, our hearts were sprinkled with Jesus' blood. As obedient Christians, we serve God from sincere hearts. Our hearts produce sacrificial gifts on earth that we bring to the Father when we die. These gifts are tested by God's fire and graded as gold, silver, or precious stones according to 1 Corinthians 3:12–15. The tested gifts are then walked to the Father under the authority of Jesus, who is High Priest over God's house.[xxxv] Since gifts come from blood-sprinkled

Tabernacle Gifts

hearts, the goat's blood was representative of gifts brought by obedient Christians.[lxxxviii]

according to the foreknowledge of God the Father, by the sanctifying work of the Spirit, to obey Jesus Christ and be sprinkled with His blood: May grace and peace be yours in the fullest measure. (1 Pet. 1:2 NASB)

The goat's blood, like the bull's blood, was sprinkled seven times before the Mercy Seat Throne. An obedient Christian, like Jesus, has the opportunity to bring seven gifts from their heart to God.[lxxxii] The following is a list of the gifts we bring to God; each one comes from a sincere heart (emphasis added to the scriptures with underline):

■ The gift of worship and prayer:

speaking to one another in psalms and hymns and spiritual songs, singing and making melody in your <u>heart</u> to the Lord, giving thanks always for all things to God the Father in the name of our Lord Jesus Christ, (Eph. 5:19–20 NKJV)

Now flee from youthful lusts and pursue righteousness, faith, love and peace, with those who call on the Lord from a pure <u>heart</u>. (2 Tim. 2:22 NASB)

Our First Day in Heaven

■ The gift of good works and sharing:

Whatever you do, work at it with all your <u>heart</u>, as working for the Lord, not for men, (Col. 3:23 NIV)

■ The gift of financial giving:

Each man should give what he has decided in his <u>heart</u> to give, not reluctantly or under compulsion, for God loves a cheerful giver. (2 Cor. 9:7 NIV)

■ The gift of love:

Now that you have purified yourselves by obeying the truth so that you have sincere love for your brothers, love one another deeply, from the <u>heart</u>. (1 Pet. 1:22 NIV)

■ The gift of fellowship and encouragement:

My purpose is that they may be encouraged in <u>heart</u> and united in love, so that they may have the full riches of complete understanding, in order that they may know the mystery of God, namely, Christ, (Col. 2:2 NIV)

Tabernacle Gifts

■ The gift of studying God's Word:

"But the seed in the good soil, these are the ones who have heard the word in an honest and good <u>heart</u>, and hold it fast, and bear fruit with perseverance. (Luke 8:15 NASB)

■ The gift of obedience:

Obey them not only to win their favor when their eye is on you, but like slaves of Christ, doing the will of God from your <u>heart</u>. (Eph. 6:6 NIV)

We will consider each of these gifts in greater detail later in this chapter.

◄ Continuing Our Walk... ►

Returning to our walk, we will continue with our gifts in hand toward the laver. Once before the laver we will wash, representing that our minds have been cleansed of sin's effects.[20] The water represents our obedient baptism[xxxvi] and the water of God's Word, which has cleansed our evil conscience. How important it is that we read the Bible daily in this life.

---

[20]*Both baptism (Rom. 6:1–14) and reading the Word represent the cleansing of our consciences (1 Pet. 3:21).*

Our First Day in Heaven

let us draw near with a sincere heart in full assurance of faith, having our hearts sprinkled clean from an evil conscience and our bodies washed with pure water. (Heb. 10:22 NASB)

We will then enter God's Tent of Meeting in heaven. There, we will be immediately aware of the amazingly sweet aroma of Jesus' incense.[lxxxiii] We ourselves will not have brought incense because our lives were not perfect. The candlestick on our left will light the way. The base (foundation) of it represents Christ. The seven branches are representative of the seven time segments of the church that Jesus established on earth. (The Lord, in Revelation 2 and 3, divided His church into seven distinct time segments, starting with the early apostolic church, called Ephesus, to the last church segment right before the rapture, called Laodicea. We, at this time period, are in the last church segment.) The light represents the Word of God, which is the Bible that we need to read so diligently on earth. The reason that both the laver and the candlelight represent His Word is due to the dual nature of the Word's ability to cleanse (wash away sin's effects) and to enlighten (bring to maturity) the Christian. The oil represents the Holy Spirit, who leads us into all truth. The Holy Spirit was also represented by the cloud pillar, which led the children of Israel to the Promised Land. He leads us to heaven.

On our right is the golden table, representative of Christ's millennial kingdom, of which we will be a

Tabernacle Gifts

part and rule with Him.[21] [xxxvii] The unleavened bread, which was renewed every seven days on the Sabbath, represents the constant nourishment we receive when our minds are renewed with the Word of God, with Christian fellowship, and with our prayer time. How important it is to attend church each Sunday. The pure incense with the unleavened bread represents the truth now present in us.

We also see that there is only one room; there is no veil. We will most likely kneel here and worship. Remember how the assistant priests could only walk in the Holy Place? They could not see, let alone go into, the Holy of Holies.[xxxviii] We will have confidence to walk into that formerly veiled second room, the Holy of Holies, which is now disclosed to us, to enjoy fellowship with God. The absence of the veil will create a boldness to continue our walk toward God's Throne. We will be confident because we know that Jesus prepared the way for us by His sacrificial gifts and that we enter with our hearts sprinkled with His blood.

Therefore, brothers, since we have confidence to enter the Most Holy Place by the blood of Jesus,

---

[21]*It is apparent that the candlestick and the golden table are opposite each other and not directly in front of us. This represents that we are looking at the same thing at different times, i.e. the church. On the left is the spiritually growing church of the present time, divided into seven time segments, and on the right, the ruling church during the millennium and ages to come (Rev. 21:9–14), divided into twelve tribes. Both are completely founded on Christ.*

Our First Day in Heaven

by a new and living way opened for us through the curtain, that is, his body, (Heb. 10:19–20 NIV)

    Before us is the golden altar, which represents our praise, worship, and prayers to God.[lxxvii] How important our quiet time is. We will stand and then pause at the golden altar to worship. God's presence fully lights the Holy of Holies. The Son of God is seated on the right hand of the Father's Mercy Seat Throne. We will step around the golden altar, lay the gifts of our sacrificial lives down, and stand[xxxix] before God. We are before the Father and the Son and the Holy Spirit alone. There will not be a crowd or other Christians present or a relative to stand with us. Each one of us will stand singularly before God and our High Priest.

So then each one of us will give an account of himself to God. (Rom. 14:12 NASB)

    We will not go before Him empty-handed. You would not want to come to God the Father without a gift. He will accept our works and reward us accordingly. This of course, has nothing to do with the issue of salvation. If we were not saved, we would not even have been allowed through the east gate. God knows us very well; we are His sons and daughters.

Now if we are children, then we are heirs—heirs of God and co-heirs with Christ, if indeed we share in his sufferings in order that we may also

share in his glory. I consider that our present sufferings are not worth comparing with the glory that will be revealed in us. The creation waits in eager expectation for the sons of God to be revealed. (Rom. 8:17–19 NIV)

Now, what do you see when you look at the tabernacle picture? Do you see your first day in heaven, your first day in His presence?

~ Tabernacle Gifts ~

Let's examine, in greater detail, the gifts we will bring to the Father. Just as the goat's blood was sprinkled seven times before the Throne, the Bible teaches us that there are seven sacrificial gifts that a New Testament Christian can bring to God. As observed previously, each of these gifts comes from our sprinkled, true hearts. Our sacrifices need to follow Jesus' seven sacrifices in order to sacrifice in the same manner and please God.[xcix] In effect, we are to do with the goat's blood as was done with the blood of the bull as required on the Day of Atonement.[xl]

Have this attitude in yourselves which was also in Christ Jesus, (Phil. 2:5 NASB)

Our First Day in Heaven

■ The sacrificial gift of worship and prayer:

Follow Jesus by understanding the difference between God and us; we are not equal: "Who, although He existed in the form of God, did not regard equality with God a thing to be grasped" (Phil. 2:6 NASB).

Jesus knew He was God, but for our sake He became a man. He fully understood the differences and voluntarily did not use or exercise certain attributes of His Glory while on earth. We need to have this same attitude in ourselves by seeking to understand the differences between God and us when we worship. Every morning take time to have private thanksgiving, worship, and prayer with God; most Christians call this "quiet time." Start by contemplating the great differences between God and mankind. Your time with Him will never be more powerful. Worship Him for those differences. Your worship and prayer time is a sacrificial gift for the Father.

Through Jesus, therefore, let us continually offer to God a <u>sacrifice</u> of praise—the fruit of lips that confess his name. (Heb. 13:15 NIV, emphasis added)

Our prayers come before God, are laid on His golden altar, and are continually before Him. Notice the following verse from Revelation:

Tabernacle Gifts

And another angel came and stood at the altar, having a golden censer; and there was given unto him much incense, that he should offer it with the prayers of all saints upon the golden altar which was before the throne. (Rev. 8:3 KJV)

The areas of worship and prayer are too great to examine completely in this book. However, the next time you pray, picture yourself coming to the Father from the tabernacle point of view. Like David, who said we should, enter through His east gate with thanksgiving and come into His court with praise.[xli] Let us continue in prayer on through the Tent of Meeting to the Holy of Holies and approach God's Throne with confidence, knowing our High Priest understands us and made the way clear, all the way to God. God will answer our prayers.

Let us then approach the throne of grace with confidence, so that we may receive mercy and find grace to help us in our time of need. (Heb. 4:16 NIV)

■ The sacrificial gift of good works and sharing:

Follow Jesus by sharing selflessly with others: "But emptied Himself"(Phil. 2:7 NASB).

Jesus emptied Himself for us by giving up the independent use of His Divine attributes, and submitted to

Our First Day in Heaven

the Father's will to save us.[xlii] We need to have this same attitude in ourselves by giving of ourselves to serve others. Visit the sick, visit those in prison, bring food to someone in need, be generous, be godly parents, be hospitable, help brothers and sisters in trouble, serve others, and do many more good deeds. Together your good works and sharing is a sacrificial gift for the Father.

And do not forget to do good and to share with others, for with such <u>sacrifices</u> God is pleased. (Heb. 13:16 NIV, emphasis added)

and is well known for her good deeds, such as bringing up children, showing hospitality, washing the feet of the saints, helping those in trouble and devoting herself to all kinds of good deeds. (1 Tim. 5:10 NIV)

■ The sacrificial gift of financial giving:

Follow Jesus by being voluntarily indebted to God: "Taking the form of a bond-servant" (Phil. 2:7 NASB).

In Old Testament times, when someone became financially indebted to another they could freely choose[22] to work off the financial obligation by

---

[22]*Exodus 21:5–6 allows a person to freely choose to become a bond-servant if he loves his master and does not wish to go free.*

Tabernacle Gifts

becoming a bond-servant. Jesus, who owed no debt, became a bond-servant to God for us by working off our debt to God. We need to have this same attitude in ourselves by also voluntarily becoming indebted to God in a financial way. Give a tithe, 10 percent of your income before it has been taxed, to the church you regularly attend. Beyond this, be generous with public ministries that God uses to bless you, such as crusades, missionaries, Christian organizations, etc. Also, be financially generous with Christians in need, or, if you are an employer, give them work.[xliii] Your financial giving is a sacrificial gift for the Father.

But I have received everything in full and have an abundance; I am amply supplied, having received from Epaphroditus what you have sent [money], a fragrant aroma, an acceptable <u>sacrifice</u>, well-pleasing to God. (Phil. 4:18 NASB, emphasis added)

This service [financial gifts] that you perform is not only supplying the needs of God's people but is also overflowing in many expressions of thanks to God. Because of the service [financial gifts] by which you have proved yourselves, men will praise God for the obedience that accompanies your confession of the gospel of Christ, and for your generosity in sharing with them and with everyone else. (2 Cor. 9:12–13 NIV)

Our First Day in Heaven

When Jesus gave the Sermon on the Mount, He taught that although the Law required that we not murder, in addition, we should not even hate. Although the Law required that we not commit adultery, we should not even lust. In this way, He encouraged us to do more than the Law ever required. In the same way, the Law required that a tithe[23] be given; Jesus is saying give that and more (see Matthew 5 and 6).

"Do not think that I came to abolish the Law or the Prophets; I did not come to abolish but to fulfill. (Matt. 5:17 NASB)

■ The sacrificial gift of love:

Follow Jesus; when you see others, see yourself and love them the way you love yourself: "And being made in the likeness of men" (Phil. 2:7 NASB).

In heaven Jesus had the likeness of God. However, Jesus loved mankind by becoming a man in flesh and blood: He looked like a man. While on

---

[23]*Actually, there were two tithes totaling 20 percent that were given each year (Lev. 27:30 and Deut. 14:22, 28). The first 10 percent was given for the regular maintenance of the priests. The second 10 percent was given in Jerusalem for the Lord's Feast. However, every third year the second 10 percent was to be kept locally and used for the poor. That is why we give the first 10 percent to our local church and gifts above that to other ministries that the Holy Spirit leads us to support and why we also give to the poor.*

earth, when Jesus looked into a mirror He no longer saw the appearance of the Glorified Son of God but instead He saw the likeness of an ordinary man.[xliv] A person will normally take care of himself or herself by making sure he or she is fed, clothed, sheltered, etc. That is why it is said people love themselves.

For no one ever hated his own flesh, but nourishes and cherishes it, just as the Lord does the church. (Eph. 5:29–30 NKJV)

The Lord took on our appearance; now when He looks at us, it is like seeing Himself as a man, and He loves us and takes care of us, as He does Himself.

We need to have this same attitude. Seeing another person as if that person were you makes it much easier to love them the way that Jesus loves you. When we do that, we can love others as we love ourselves.

Owe nothing to anyone except to love one another; for he who loves his neighbor has fulfilled the law. For this, "YOU SHALL NOT COMMIT ADULTERY, YOU SHALL NOT MURDER, YOU SHALL NOT STEAL, YOU SHALL NOT COVET," and if there is any other commandment, it is summed up in this saying, "YOU SHALL LOVE YOUR NEIGHBOR AS YOURSELF." (Rom. 13:8–9 NASB)

Our First Day in Heaven

We are to love other Christians and be devoted to one another in brotherly love. Do not be prideful, but be willing to associate with people of low position. Love sacrificially the Christian you are sitting next to in church, as much as you love yourself. We are to love the unsaved by bringing them the good news of the gospel through evangelism. Often, to love others as ourselves requires hardship on our part. Both the apostle Paul and the apostle John tell us that a Christian's life spent in sacrificial love is called our "walk in love." We need to follow Christ's example of sacrificial love and love others as we love ourselves. Your "walk in love" is a sacrificial gift for the Father.

and walk in love, just as Christ also loved you and gave Himself up for us, an offering and a <u>sacrifice</u> to God as a fragrant aroma. (Eph. 5:2 NIV, emphasis added)

And this is love: that we walk in obedience to his commands. As you have heard from the beginning, his command is that you walk in love. (2 John 6 NIV)

■ The sacrificial gift of fellowship and encouragement:

Follow Jesus by being found with other Christians: "Being found in appearance as a man" (Phil. 2:8 NASB).

Tabernacle Gifts

Jesus not only became a man, but He also left heaven and lived with mankind and adopted mankind's ways of eating, sleeping, etc. In all respects and appearances, He was found living as a man. We need to have this same attitude in ourselves and also be found living our lives with other Christians. Fellowship with other Christians daily. Attend a local church or fellowship regularly; do not give up this time of meeting together. Use this time to spur one another on and to encourage one another.

We will never be such mature Christians that we no longer need to attend church. If you don't attend church for your own growth, attend for the benefit of encouraging others. Sacrifice your time and become a church leader, deacon, Bible study teacher, choir member, someone who points out God's way to others, or serve on church committees. When you do these things, you are sacrificing yourself for the benefit of others' faith. Your fellowship and encouragement for the benefit of other Christians is a sacrificial gift for the Father.

Yea, and if I be offered upon the <u>sacrifice</u> and service of your faith, I joy, and rejoice with you all. (Phil. 2:17 KJV, emphasis added)

And let us consider how we may spur one another on toward love and good deeds. Let us not give up meeting together, as some are in the habit of doing, but let us encourage one another—and all

Our First Day in Heaven

the more as you see the Day approaching. **(Heb. 10:24–25 NIV)**

■ The sacrificial gift of studying God's Word:

Follow Jesus by humbly accepting God's instruction and direction: "He humbled Himself"(Phil. 2:8 NASB).

Jesus humbled himself to be trained by God. Although He was the all-knowing and always obedient Son of God, Jesus humbly *learned* obedience from His suffering.

Although He was a Son, He learned obedience from the things which He suffered. (Heb. 5:8 NASB)

We need to have this same humble attitude and allow ourselves to be trained by God. Jesus asks us to learn from Him by humbly putting on His yoke and reminds us that He is also humble.

"Take My yoke upon you and learn from Me, for I am gentle and humble in heart, and YOU WILL FIND REST FOR YOUR SOULS. (Matt. 11:29 NASB)

We have this attitude in ourselves when we accept instruction and direction from God's Word. Reading God's Word is learning from Jesus and

Tabernacle Gifts

putting on His yoke; in fact, Jesus is called "The Word of God."

He is clothed with a robe dipped in blood, and His name is called The Word of God. (Rev. 19:13 NASB)

By reading the Bible we are cleansing the old sinful mind and replacing it with the truth. In the Bible, sin is represented by yeast (leaven) in bread and unleavened bread represents the absence of sin. However, that is not enough; to be holy, we must also replace sin with truth. That is why the unleavened bread in the tabernacle was also placed on the table along with pure incense. The pure incense represents truth within the believer. In order to make unleavened bread, you have to throw out or sacrifice the yeast. The Jews celebrate Passover with unleavened bread. Jesus is our Passover. He was sacrificed for us. He took on sin (leaven) and was thrown out (sacrificed) for our benefit. We are to sacrifice the yeast or sin that is in our life and replace it with unleavened bread and truth, which is the Word of God. Your time studying God's Word is a sacrificial gift for the Father.

Purge out therefore the old leaven, that ye may be a new lump, as ye are unleavened. For even Christ our passover is <u>sacrificed</u> for us: Therefore let us keep the feast, not with old leaven, neither with the leaven of malice and wicked-

Our First Day in Heaven

ness; but with the unleavened bread of sincerity and truth. (1 Cor. 5:7–8 KJV, emphasis added)

Remember the dual nature of the Word's ability both to cleanse sin's effects and to bring us to maturity. Maturity comes from reading the Word of God. If all we ever speak about are the basics regarding Christ, we are only drinking milk like infants and not moving on to solid food.

For everyone who partakes only of milk is not accustomed to the word of righteousness [the Bible], for he is an infant. But solid food [deeper truth] is for the mature, who because of practice [study the Bible] have their senses trained to discern good and evil. (Heb. 5:13–14 NASB)

By sacrificing your time to read and study the Bible, you are humbling yourself, through cleansing the old sinful mind and through enlightenment in the knowledge of God, to do good works for God. The Word teaches, rebukes, corrects, and trains you. The Word of God equips you with the knowledge of what God will have you do and how and when to do it.

All Scripture is God-breathed and is useful for teaching, rebuking, correcting and training in righteousness, so that the man of God may be thoroughly equipped for every good work. (2 Tim. 3:16–17 NIV)

Tabernacle Gifts

Perhaps you think the Bible is too difficult to understand or that you have to go to seminary to be taught its meanings. That is what the Pharisees stated to Jesus. They wanted to know how He taught them the Scriptures when He did not go to school for this knowledge. Jesus told them the Father revealed it. The Holy Spirit will also reveal the meaning of His Word to you, when you study it.

And the Jews marveled, saying, "How does this Man know letters, having never studied?" Jesus answered them and said, "My doctrine is not Mine, but His who sent Me. (John 7:15–16 NKJV)

■ The sacrificial gift of obedience:

Follow Jesus by obeying God completely: "By becoming obedient to the point of death, even death on a cross" (Phil. 2:8 NASB).

Jesus was the immortal Son of God who never had to die like a mortal man. However, not only did He obey God and die, He died a shameful death. We need to have this same attitude in ourselves by also obeying God. The greatest gift you can bring is your obedience to God's will, which is the sacrifice of your will.

The Old Testament contained animal sacrifices under the old covenant. However, Jesus knew that these sacrifices, although required by the old covenant (the Law), did not satisfy God. God really

Our First Day in Heaven

preferred obedience. So Jesus said, rather than do these types of sacrifices, He would sacrifice by doing God's will. When He said this, He set aside the old way to sacrifice and established a new way to sacrifice called obedience. Jesus sacrificed His will to live, to be obedient to God. This kind of obedience always produces great gifts for God. In Jesus' case, His sacrifice made us holy. Your obedience is a sacrificial gift for the Father.

First he said, "Sacrifices and offerings, burnt offerings and sin offerings you did not desire, nor were you pleased with them" (although the law required them to be made). Then he said, "Here I am, I have come to do your will." He sets aside the first to establish the second. And by that will, we have been made holy through the <u>sacrifice</u> of the body of Jesus Christ once for all. (Heb. 10:8–10 NIV, emphasis added).

We have to know God's will before we can do it. The Word of God, fellowship, and prayer renew our minds to know His will.

And do not be conformed to this world, but be transformed by the renewing of your mind, so that you may prove what the will of God is, that which is good and acceptable and perfect. (Rom. 12:2 NASB)

Tabernacle Gifts

Jesus also read the Word of God and He obediently responded—He read what He was asked by God to do and He agreed to do it.

Then I said, 'Here I am-it is written about me in the scroll- I have come to do your will, O God.'" (Heb. 10:7 NIV)[24]

Once you know God's will, do it obediently. Obey God with joy, not reluctantly. It is your eagerness in doing His will that pleases Him. No other gift is as powerful as this. Nor will any other gift be as valuable to Him.

These seven New Testament sacrifices will survive the fire of God's altar.

Your gifts will simply stand on their own and represent your sacrificial walk with God after your salvation. Your gifts are not limited or qualified by your former sinful life, because God promised to remember your sins no more.

I thank Christ Jesus our Lord, who has given me strength, that he considered me faithful, appointing me to his service. Even though I was once a blasphemer and a persecutor and a violent man,

---

[24]*The scroll Jesus is referring to is the Scriptures of the Old Testament, kept on scrolls at that time. One of those, Leviticus 16, speaks about what He would do in detail; see Appendix A for a verse-by-verse commentary on this chapter.*

Our First Day in Heaven

I was shown mercy because I acted in ignorance and unbelief. (1 Tim. 1:12–13 NIV)

When we present our gifts before God's Throne we will not be afraid because we are royal priests in the order of the Royal High Priest. We are allowed in the Holy of Holies because Jesus' sacrificial gifts removed the veil.

⁀ Follow Him outside ⁀ the Camp

Remember the assistant priests who brought out the rejected parts of the bull and goat and walked past thousands of people? What did they represent? It is believed the people in the camp represented the unsaved world.[lxxviii]

When Jesus was crucified, He was taken outside the city gates and hung shamefully on a cross. Obedient Christians are to take up their cross and follow Him. Jesus endured the shame and rejection of the world. We are to follow His example. Just as the rejected parts of the goat followed the rejected parts of the bull, we are to follow Jesus outside the camp.

For the bodies of those animals, whose blood is brought into the sanctuary by the high priest for sin, are burned outside the camp. Therefore

Tabernacle Gifts

Jesus also, that He might sanctify the people with His own blood, suffered outside the gate. Therefore let us go forth to Him, outside the camp, bearing His reproach. (Heb. 13:11–13 NKJV)

The world follows money, the stock market, fame, pleasure, and whoever is considered rich or powerful. We follow a man who died; that is shameful and foolish to the world. We know it is wisdom. The man who died is the Son of the Living God made flesh, who was raised from death by the Father and is now seated in heavenly places with God and is the King of kings and Lord of lords.

When the world hates you, laughs at you, or rejects you for going to choir practice, reading your Bible on an airplane, witnessing, or trusting God by tithing, you will know that you are following Him outside the camp. The people of the camp looked away from those rejected remains.

The Scapegoat

What did the scapegoat represent? The scapegoat symbolized the lack of sacrifice.[25] It represented the absence of sacrifice in certain Christians. Christians who become saved but because they are too busy with worldly things or just lazy, do little or nothing with their salvation. They have no sacrifice, little service, few good deeds, and little spiritual growth.

Our First Day in Heaven

They seldom read the Bible, they seldom fellowship with other Christians, they do not tithe, they seldom pray, they do little to help or show love to their Christian brothers or sisters, they rarely witness, and they do not obey. They are saved, but the fire of God's altar reveals that they have no gift to lay before God's Throne. However, they are saved.

Now if any man builds on the foundation with gold, silver, precious stones, wood, hay, straw, each man's work will become evident; for the day will show it because it is to be revealed with fire, and the fire itself will test the quality of each man's work. If any man's work which he has built on it remains, he will receive a reward. If any man's work is burned up, he will suffer loss; but he himself will be saved, yet so as through fire. (1 Cor. 3:12–15 NASB)

We all know such Christians who do very little or nothing for the Kingdom of God. Often, all their work is for the kingdom of money.[xlv] These Christians wander from the truth.

---

[25]*Many Bible commentators differ on the interpretation of the meaning of the two goats. Many believe that the sacrificial goat, as well as the bull, represents the work of Christ. They also believe that the scapegoat represents either Christ or an evil spirit or sin, which is separated from us. Regardless of the meaning of the goats, the message in Hebrews 6:19–20 and 13:11–14, which is "we Christians are to follow the example of Jesus' sacrificial life," is not affected. See Appendix B at the back of this book for FAQs.*

Tabernacle Gifts

My brothers, if one of you should wander from the truth and someone should bring him back, (James 5:19 NIV)

They enjoy their salvation but will have nothing to present to the Father. What little they do is to be seen of men, in which case this false work will be burned on God's altar and revealed to be wood, hay, and straw. In Luke 19:11–27, Jesus describes four different groups or individuals in the parable of the money usage. First, He describes those who totally refused to do the will of the nobleman; these he ordered killed, representing the unsaved. Next, He describes the nobleman's good servants. The nobleman gave each of his servants one mina (a mina is equal to one hundred days' wages). One servant made ten times more; another servant made five times more. Both represent the varied amount of gifts brought by mature obedient Christians to God. Finally, the last servant, who also was given one mina, made nothing. He represents the scapegoat (lazy) Christian; the nobleman took his mina away and gave it to the one with ten minas but did not kill this servant.

The throwing of lots over the goats indicates the Christian's free will to choose a sacrificial life or to choose a life with little service to God. This is not something God chooses; the choice will be made by us.[lxxxiv] However, God does grant mercy to us, by revealing to us His will.

The man walking the scapegoat outside the camp was not someone the people looked away from,

Our First Day in Heaven

unlike the assistant priests who brought out the rejected parts. He was just a man walking a live goat, probably a common sight. A priest did not walk the goat to the wilderness, but most probably a non-priest Levite. In the same way those scapegoat (lazy)[lxxxv] Christians, who never let anyone in the world see that they are Christian for fear the world will reject them and thus they will make less money, take a different path. These undercover Christians are very acceptable to the world. These Christians grow somewhat weary of serving God and lose heart bearing the shame of the cross (witnessing).

Consider him who endured such opposition from sinful men, so that you will not grow weary and lose heart. (Heb. 12:3 NIV)

How do you think you would feel if you were a rich Christian in this life, but when you arrived in heaven you had nothing to bring to the Father? What if you had few righteous acts and did not struggle hard[lxxxvi] against sin? Will you even have a white robe to wear? When Jesus described each time segment of His church, He gave the last time segment, the one in which we are living, a very grave description and admonition. He said to the *Christians* of our time:

You say, 'I am rich; I have acquired wealth and do not need a thing.' But you do not realize that you are wretched, pitiful, poor, blind and naked. I

Tabernacle Gifts

counsel you to buy from me gold refined in the fire, so you can become rich; and white clothes to wear, so you can cover your shameful nakedness; and salve to put on your eyes, so you can see. (Rev. 3:17–18 NIV)

    To fully understand the above verses, let's look at the key words in a fuller context.

    Jesus said to today's scapegoat Christian of this last time-segment church [*You*] will be rich and prideful [*I am rich, I have acquired*]. However, you do not realize [*do not realize*] that true riches will only be determined in the true tabernacle. There you are considered unwashed by the Word [*wretched*], unfed by fellowship, prayer, or the Word [*pitiful*] and without gifts [*poor*]. You are considered blind [*blind*] because you do not obey the leading of His Word or the leading of the Holy Spirit. You are also still sinning and not serving [*naked*]. Jesus said, consider using your free will [*I counsel*] to sacrifice [*buy*]. By following Me [*from Me*] you will obtain the kind of works and service, which renders gold, after it is placed on God's altar [*gold refined in the fire*]. In this way you will have gifts for the Father [*become rich*] and put away sin [*white robe to wear*], because you were instead serving [*cover your shameful nakedness*]. You will now be able to obey the leading of the Holy Spirit [*salve to put on your eyes*] and be able to see your way and not wander [*you can see*].

    How useless to not have used a sprinkled heart to produce gifts for God. However, it is interesting to

Our First Day in Heaven

notice that despite His scathing assessment of scapegoat Christians, He is still providing them with the opportunity to change and end up with wonderful gifts for the Father.[lxxxvii]

The Old Testament picture of assistant priests and non-priest Levites was designed to be an example of how we are to live today. Remember we learned that all priests were Levites, but not all Levites were priests. All Christians are designated by God to be assistant priests. However, Christians have a choice to *act* like assistant priests[lxxxviii] on earth or to ignore their priestly duties and *act* like non-priests.[lxxxix] It could be said, "All Christians are priests, but not all Christians act like priests."

What happens to these scapegoat (non-priestly acting) Christians in heaven? When do they stand before God? What type of repayment will they incur, as mentioned in Colossians 3:25? What type of loss do they suffer? These questions go beyond the search of this book. The important point is we are not to live that way. We are to live as sacrificial Christians.

⁀ The Ram Sacrifice ⁀

As we observed, the rams represented the results of Christ's work. The first ram, brought[xc] with the bull, represented the first half of His results: the Old Testament righteous, finally brought before God. The second ram, brought with the goats, represented the

Tabernacle Gifts

second half of His results: the New Testament Christians. When the whole rams were sacrificed at the end of the day, they represented a yet-to-occur event, when all of God's people will be in heaven. At that time no saint will be left out (no rejected part). On that day, the true High Priest will present the results of all His work to God: the Old and New Testament saints! Now that will be a celebration. At the time of the ram offering, the earthly high priest also placed some of the fat of the bull and goat on the altar. This represented the joy of our High Priest. Could Psalm 66 be the very words that Christ uses on that day?[xlvi]

I will offer You burnt sacrifices of fat animals, With the sweet aroma of rams; I will offer bulls with goats. (Ps. 66:15 NKJV)

⁌ Our Search Complete ⁌

Now that we have examined the meaning of the tabernacle and the Day of Atonement, let's go over the main points. The tabernacle on earth represented the true tabernacle, heaven. The Hebrew Day of Atonement is actually heaven's holiest ceremony, which started with Jesus' triumphant return and will end when the last sacrificial Christians place their gifts before God and Christ. The high priest represented Jesus, the true High Priest. The bull's blood repre-

Our First Day in Heaven

sented Jesus' sacrifices, of which there were seven. The first ram, brought in with the bull, represented the first half of the results of Jesus' work: the Old Testament righteous. The assistant priests, who were allowed to serve in the Tent of Meeting, represented obedient Christians. The sacrificial goat's blood represented the sacrifices of these Christians. Obedient Christians also have seven sacrifices, which follow Christ's sacrifices. The non-priest Levites represented the behavior of non-sacrificial Christians. The non-priest Levites had no service in the Tent of Meeting; however, they were allowed to work in the court. The scapegoat represented the absence of sacrifice on the part of these non-sacrificial Christians. The second ram, brought in with the goats, represented the second half of the results of Jesus' work: the New Testament Christians. The camp represented the unsaved people in the world, who will never be allowed in God's house. The children of Israel waiting for Aaron represented the Old Testament righteous, prior to Jesus' atonement, who were finally allowed to enter into God's rest.

Chapter 7

∽ Be Encouraged! ∾

Jesus knows the great pressure that we are all under in this society to succeed financially. He knows the astonishing pressure we receive from the media, TV, and Hollywood to conform to the world's view of success.

Therefore, Jesus made an incredible promise to all Christians of our time who do serve Him and are not scapegoat (lazy) Christians. He said if you overcome[26] the deceitfulness of worldly wealth in your time and instead live a sacrificial life for Him, He will let you *sit down*, in the Holy of Holies, on His Throne (shared with the Father) just like He sat down on His Father's Throne.

---

[26] This statement follows the verses in Revelation 3:17–18 which we studied earlier under the scapegoat.

Tabernacle Gifts

He who overcomes, I will grant to him to sit down with Me on My throne, as I also overcame and sat down with My Father on His throne. (Rev. 3:21 NASB)

This extraordinary promise is hard to believe! Can we be so privileged through our sacrificial lives to actually receive such a place on God's Mercy Seat Throne? Will there be room to sit? Of course, we are speaking of heavenly things, not earthly. Besides literally sitting down, we will rule His creation with Him. To reign with Christ! Glory to God! There is no one like Jesus! All praise is given to the Amen, the faithful and true Witness, the Ruler of God's creation, Jesus, the Son of God.

This unique promise, which is far better than any wealth accumulated on earth, lasts for eternity, and is our incredible reward for overcoming. This promise is for all overcoming, sacrificial, and obedient Christians of our time-period church (Laodicea).

You are not a scapegoat Christian; you are studying the Scripture verses in this book aren't you?

Continue to follow God's command to do good works and to be generous! You will bring a rich treasure to the Father and be rewarded in the true life, which will come in heaven. Strive to make your sacrifices more of gold than silver in quality.[27]

---

[27] *First Corinthians 3:12–15 lists the grade of gifts we bring in descending order, i.e. gold, silver, precious stones. (Man can now make precious stones like diamonds.)*

Be Encouraged!

Command them to do good, to be rich in good deeds, and to be generous and willing to share. In this way they will lay up treasure for themselves as a firm foundation for the coming age, so that they may take hold of the life that is truly life. (1 Tim. 6:18–19 NIV)

Perhaps now we better understand why so much of God's Word is dedicated to this tabernacle picture. Perhaps also we have obtained an understanding of the relevance of this picture to our current mature Christian lives. We may even have improved our appreciation of why we sacrifice for Christ's sake, to bring our gifts to the Father. We may understand better why we are called kings and priests, because we minister as priests to God with our sacrificial gifts and we will reign as kings with Christ forever.

Focus on Jesus as your example, obey Him and He will make your gifts acceptable. Know that all your good works will not be forgotten, so do not grow weary and cease to do them.

Let us fix our eyes on Jesus, the author and perfecter of our faith, who for the joy set before him endured the cross, scorning its shame, and sat down at the right hand of the throne of God. Consider him who endured such opposition from sinful men, so that you will not grow weary and lose heart. (Heb. 12:2–3 NIV)

Tabernacle Gifts

God is not unjust; he will not forget your work and the love you have shown him as you have helped his people and continue to help them. We want each of you to show this same diligence to the very end, in order to make your hope sure. We do not want you to become lazy, but to imitate those who through faith and patience inherit what has been promised. (Heb. 6:10–12 NIV)

Hopefully, through a better understanding, you are encouraged to continue all the work you have already been doing. Continue to have a bold confidence in your prayers and a readiness for heaven, due to the opening of the way by our Royal High Priest over God's house. Continue to serve God from a sincere heart, which has been sprinkled with Jesus' blood. Continue to wash and enlighten your mind with the reading of the Word each day. Continue unswervingly to bear His reproach and to follow Him. Continue to walk in love. Continue in your good works, giving and fellowship. Continue in your obedience. Do not fail to overcome by remembering His incredible Throne promise, you kings and priests of the Lord.

Therefore, brothers, since we have confidence to enter the Most Holy Place by the blood of Jesus, by a new and living way opened for us through the curtain, that is, his body, and since we have a great priest over the house of God, let us draw near to God with a sincere heart in full assurance

Be Encouraged!

of faith, having our hearts sprinkled to cleanse us from a guilty conscience and having our bodies washed with pure water. Let us hold unswervingly to the hope we profess, for he who promised is faithful. And let us consider how we may spur one another on toward love and good deeds. Let us not give up meeting together, as some are in the habit of doing, but let us encourage one another-and all the more as you see the Day approaching. (Heb. 10:19–25 NIV)

May your tabernacle gifts be abundant that Day when you see Him!

Epilogue

~ His Greatness Is ~ Unsearchable!

We will spend all of eternity searching out the greatness of God.

Great is the LORD**, and greatly to be praised; And His greatness is unsearchable. (Ps. 145:3 NKJV)**

One question often begs another. Each answered question from God's Word piques our interest and creates another question. Each time we open God's Word, we mature. In this epilogue we will search out just a few more answers. Before we start our first day in heaven and present our gifts, we must first enter through heaven's east gate. What will we face there?

Tabernacle Gifts

~ The Angel Guards at ~ Heaven's Gate

Heaven's gate is closed and guarded by angels, with strict orders not to let in anyone who is not approved. Will they let us pass? Let's first see what these guards did when Jesus entered heaven. The sight of Jesus bringing all the Old Testament righteous from Sheol and approaching the gate should have been overwhelming to the angel guards. Yet they did not have the gate open. Why? Let's first understand a little more about this gate and the angels guarding it.

This gate does not look like the pearl gate described in Revelation 21 and 22. That gate is part of the new heaven, which will actually have twelve pearl gates, open all of the time.

On no day will its gates ever be shut, for there will be no night there. (Rev. 21:25–26 NIV)

The gate we will face is the gate of heaven that exists now. This gate is shut tightly and is guarded,[xci] especially after a third[xlvii] of the angels in heaven rebelled against God.

Jacob saw angels and heaven's gate in a dream and became afraid. He observed that stairs from earth to heaven precede this gate. There are also many angels present traveling between heaven and earth, on assignments.[xlviii]

Epilogue

He had a dream in which he saw a stairway resting on the earth, with its top reaching to heaven, and the angels of God were ascending and descending on it. (Gen. 28:12 NIV)

He was afraid and said, "How awesome is this place! This is none other than the house of God, and this is the gate of heaven." (Gen. 28:17 NASB)

Ezekiel also saw a vision of angels traveling between the earth and heaven. He identified them as cherubim, which are the type of angels God uses as guards (the cherubim were used to guard the tree of life).[xlix] In fact, the angels he saw arrived at heaven's east gate and stood still, which meant that they were guarding it.

When the cherubim departed, they lifted their wings and rose up from the earth in my sight with the wheels beside them; and they stood still at the entrance of the east gate of the LORD's house, and the glory of the God of Israel hovered over them. (Ezek. 10:19 NASB)

When not in human form, cherubim do not look the way most artists have portrayed them. For example, in Revelation, the apostle John saw a vision of one of God's warrior angels most likely a cherub, the type that would be guarding the gate. He gives us a clear description of what a warrior angel looks like.

Tabernacle Gifts

I saw another strong angel coming down out of heaven, clothed with a cloud; and the rainbow was upon his head, and his face was like the sun, and his feet like pillars of fire; (Rev. 10:1 NASB)

and he cried out with a loud voice, as when a lion roars; and when he had cried out, the seven peals of thunder uttered their voices. (Rev. 10:3 NASB)

It is understandable why Jacob was afraid. The warrior angel described was so huge that a cloud was his cloak. He had a rainbow helmet (remember the rainbow is God's bow,[l] a weapon). The angel's face looked like the hot core of the sun, and his feet were two pillars of fire! When the warrior angel spoke, it was very loud and sounded like a lion roaring! Only one warrior like that would be needed to guard a gate, but Jacob saw many. You could not get past these guards! No one could prevail against these angel guards, not even other angels.[li]

As Jesus and the Old Testament righteous returned from Sheol and approached heaven's east gate, the procession called out to the angels guarding the gate. They asked the angels to open heaven's gate and explained that they were with Jesus, the King of Glory, and that He wished to come in.

Lift up your heads, O gates, And be lifted up, O ancient doors, That the King of glory may come in! (Ps. 24:7 NASB)

Epilogue

The angel guards roared back a question, asking them to identify this King.

Who is this King of glory? (Ps. 24:8 NKJV)

The Old Testament righteous, probably shocked, shouted back a clear description of Jesus. They said something like; "He is the LORD who defeated all His enemies at Calvary, the LORD strong and mighty, the LORD mighty in battle."

The LORD strong and mighty, The LORD mighty in battle. (Ps. 24:8 NKJV)

The righteous demanded a second time that the angels open heaven's gate so that the King could enter.

Lift up your heads, O gates, And lift them up, O ancient doors, That the King of glory may come in! (Ps. 24:9 NASB)

Surprisingly, the angel guards still did not open the gate. Instead, they roared again and repeated their question, which meant they required a better reason something like saying, "Who exactly is this King?" Perhaps also they were using these questions to "buy some time" to check with angels having higher authority.

Who is this King of glory? (Ps. 24:10 NKJV)

Tabernacle Gifts

You see for a short time, Jesus even allowed Himself to be placed a little lower then the angels, in order for Him to redeem us.

But we see Jesus, who was made a little lower than the angels, for the suffering of death crowned with glory and honor, that He, by the grace of God, might taste death for everyone. (Heb. 2:9 NKJV)

The description of Jesus' victory at Calvary given by the Old Testament righteous did not mean to these angel guards what it means to us. Christ did not die for angels; He died only for us.

For assuredly He does not give help to angels, but He gives help to the descendant of Abraham. (Heb. 2:16 NASB)

Realizing this, the multitude, with no remaining patience (think of Abraham, Sarah, Joseph, Moses, Ruth, David, Esther, and many more) in great authority ROARED back.

The LORD of hosts, He is the King of glory. (Ps. 24:10 NKJV)

They were saying to these warrior angel guards that He is also the LORD of all angelic hosts, meaning, "HE IS YOUR KING; NOW, OPEN THE GATE!" At that, the doors of this ancient gate were opened

Epilogue

wide. Jesus the KING of kings and LORD of lords, and the KING of all angels, entered heaven, followed by a multitude.

Why did the angels listen to the righteous and regard Jesus as their King? Because God has appointed Christians (which they now were) to teach angels.

to the intent that now the manifold wisdom of God might be made known by the church to the principalities and powers in the heavenly places, (Eph. 3:10 NKJV)

Jesus' exaltations included his complete superiority and subjection of all angels.

The Son is the radiance of God's glory and the exact representation of his being, sustaining all things by his powerful word. After he had provided purification for sins, he sat down at the right hand of the Majesty in heaven. So he became as much superior to the angels as the name he has inherited is superior to theirs. (Heb. 1:3–4 NIV)

who has gone into heaven and is at the right hand of God, angels and authorities and powers having been made subject to Him. (1 Pet. 3:22 NKJV)

In addition, holy angels are sent to serve Christians.

Tabernacle Gifts

Are not all angels ministering spirits sent to serve those who will inherit salvation? (Heb. 1:14 NIV)

Remember when we earlier learned that the rams (sheep) were walked into the court by the high priest and the assistant priests, along with the other animals, on the Hebrew Day of Atonement? They represented the results of Jesus' work, the Old Testament righteous and the New Testament Christians.[xcii]

Notice in the following verse, Jesus was explaining this to His disciples. He explained that in addition to bringing the New Testament Christians who were listening to Him (and still listen to Him), it was also His responsibility to bring the Old Testament righteous to heaven.[xciii] The Old Testament righteous were not currently in the world,[xciv] but at that time were still in Sheol (a different sheep pen). He also explained that in heaven He would combine both flocks: the Old and New Testament saints!

I have other sheep that are not of this sheep pen. I must bring them also. They too will listen to my voice, and there shall be one flock and one shepherd. (John 10:16 NIV)

Can you almost hear the Old Testament righteous, as they walked through the gate, singing the words from Psalm 118?

Open to me the gates of righteousness; I shall enter through them, I shall give thanks to the

Epilogue

LORD. This is the gate of the LORD; The righteous will enter through it. I shall give thanks to You, for You have answered me, And You have become my salvation. (Ps. 118:19–21 NASB)

The LORD is God, and he has made his light shine upon us. With boughs in hand, join in the festal procession up to the horns of the altar. (Ps. 118:27 NIV)

Can you imagine what Moses was thinking when he walked into the true tabernacle?

What happens when Christians reach this gate? We are approved to enter heaven's gate because we accepted Jesus as our personal King and Savior. This is the only way in. Certainly, no one could prevail against the guards. The angel guards will never let anyone not pre-approved by Jesus (their King) through the gate. They will not roar at one of King Jesus' servants, "STAND BACK FROM THE GATE!"

When we confessed Jesus as Lord and Savior and believed God raised Him from the dead, King Jesus put us on the approval list. Are you on this list? If not, now is the time to confess Jesus as your personal King and Savior. The list is updated constantly and sent to the angels guarding the gate.[xcv] Since Jesus is the only way to gain entry, He is actually referred to as the Gate. When we die and then ascend the stairs to heaven's gate, escorted by our[lii] angel, (as described in Luke 16:22) we will be recognized, accepted, and the angel guards will open the doors

Tabernacle Gifts

and let us pass. What will you be thinking? What will you be singing?

Therefore Jesus said again, "I tell you the truth, I am the gate for the sheep. (John 10:7 NIV)

I am the gate; whoever enters through me will be saved. He will come in and go out, and find pasture. (John 10:9 NIV)

Our LORD Jesus, heaven's Gate, Way through the veil, Ark, True High Priest, Exalted One, Ruler of all creation, Son of God, reign forever!

Appendix A

~ Commentary on ~ Leviticus 16[28]

16:1 And the Lord spake unto Moses after the death of the two sons of Aaron, when they offered before the Lord, and died;

God lit the altar with His fire from heaven. That same fire was to be the only fire used. Aaron's sons did not use that fire to light the censers with the holy incense; therefore, they died. The message is that only God's fire tests the lives of all men. There is no life that will not be tested by God's fire.

16:2 And the Lord said unto Moses, Speak unto Aaron thy brother, that he come not at all times into the holy place within the vail [veil] before the

---

[28] All scriptures in this appendix are from the King James Version.

Tabernacle Gifts

mercy seat, which is upon the ark; that he die not: for I will appear in the cloud upon the mercy seat.

God is Holy; no one can approach God without the blood of Christ. Christ will only have to do this once.

16:3 Thus shall Aaron come into the holy place: with a young bullock for a sin offering, and a ram for a burnt offering.

The true High Priest will enter heaven with His own blood; the complete work of salvation. The results of His work will come in two parts. The first part He will bring with Him, a gift for God of all the Old Testament righteous, represented by the ram.

16:4 He shall put on the holy linen coat, and he shall have the linen breeches upon his flesh, and shall be girded with a linen girdle, and with the linen mitre shall he be attired: these are holy garments; therefore shall he wash his flesh in water, and so put them on.

Jesus will be clothed in humanity. However, His life will be perfect, represented by white. The washing of the entire body indicates the change in nature from the Divine Glory to humanity.[xcvi]

16:5 And he shall take of the congregation of the children of Israel two kids of the goats for a sin offering, and one ram for a burnt offering.

Appendix A

The goats represented the gifts, or as we will see, lack of gifts of Christians. The ram represented that this is the second part of the results of His work, the New Testament Christians, and a gift for God.

16:6 And Aaron shall offer his bullock of the sin offering, which is for himself, and make an atonement for himself, and for his house.

Jesus alone will die a sacrificial death on the cross in order to be able to atone for the sins of the people.

16:7 And he shall take the two goats, and present them before the Lord at the door of the tabernacle of the congregation.

The gifts of the New Testament Christians will come to God by the express permission, authority, and presence of Jesus, who acknowledges His own to the Father.

16:8 And Aaron shall cast lots upon the two goats; one lot for the Lord, and the other lot for the scapegoat."

All New Testament Christian works will be tested. The sacrifices that they made or did not make were a result of their own free will.

16:9 And Aaron shall bring the goat upon which the Lord's lot fell, and offer him for a sin offering.

Tabernacle Gifts

Jesus will allow all gifts of the New Testament Christians to be tested by God's altar fire. Gifts remaining after the fire tests them will be from sacrificial Christians. If the test reveals wood, hay, or straw, nothing will remain, no sacrifice.

16:10 But the goat, on which the lot fell to be the scapegoat, shall be presented alive before the Lord, to make an atonement with him, and to let him go for a scapegoat into the wilderness.

The lack of gifts brought by certain Christians will result in certain consequences. Jesus will not allow this type of Christian to come before the Father empty-handed. All Christians are to share in Christ's work (Col. 1:24). However, the sins of these Christians were clearly forgotten.

16:11 And Aaron shall bring the bullock of the sin offering, which is for himself, and shall make an atonement for himself, and for his house, and shall kill the bullock of the sin offering which is for himself:

Jesus is sacrificed for the sins of the whole world. It is His blood.

16:12 And he shall take a censer full of burning coals of fire from off the altar before the Lord, and his hands full of sweet incense beaten small, and bring it within the vail [veil]:

Appendix A

Jesus uses the correct fire in the censer. God alone will test the quality of His life and work. The two handfuls represent that He completed all His perfect work in every respect; He could gather in His hands no more. He will now enter the Holy of Holies.

16:13 And he shall put the incense upon the fire before the Lord, that the cloud of the incense may cover the mercy seat that is upon the testimony, that he die not:

When Jesus is in the Holy of Holies He burns the incense using the fire coals from God's altar. Jesus' perfect life and work will now be put to the test. His perfect life is judged by God to be Holy. He is accepted as the true appointed High Priest.

16:14 And he shall take of the blood of the bullock, and sprinkle it with his finger upon the mercy seat eastward; and before the mercy seat shall he sprinkle of the blood with his finger seven times.

Jesus now stands before God and places His seven gifts, listed in Philippians 2:6–8. He uses His own blood, which He sprinkles seven times in the sign of His cross.

16:15 Then shall he kill the goat of the sin offering, that is for the people, and bring his blood

Tabernacle Gifts

within the vail [veil], and do with that blood as he did with the blood of the bullock, and sprinkle it upon the mercy seat, and before the mercy seat:

By the express permission and authority of the High Priest over the house of God, all Christians will be allowed to have their works tested by God's fire. Those gifts remaining will be permitted for presentation to the Father under Jesus' High Priest authority. The gifts remaining will be those that follow the example of Jesus' sacrifices (Phil. 2:5; 1 Pet. 2:21; John 13:15–17). These gifts will also be of varying quality, i.e. gold, silver, precious stones. If the gifts of some burn off like wood, hay, and straw, those Christians have no gift (scapegoat). The goat's blood is representative of Jesus' blood. Jesus' blood was sprinkled on the hearts of Christians when they were saved. It is from a sincere heart that gifts are produced on the earth and then brought to God.

16:16 And he shall make an atonement for the holy place, because of the uncleanness of the children of Israel, and because of their transgressions in all their sins: and so shall he do for the tabernacle of the congregation, that remaineth among them in the midst of their uncleanness.

The veil in heaven is removed. The Tent of Meeting will become one room. All of the Tent of Meeting is now the Holy of Holies; this allows Christians access to God.

Appendix A

16:17 And there shall be no man in the tabernacle of the congregation when he goeth in to make an atonement in the holy place, until he come out, and have made an atonement for himself, and for his household, and for all the congregation of Israel.

No one could go before the Father until Jesus made atonement for him or her. All need to wait for Jesus to be the first of many.

16:18 And he shall go out unto the altar that is before the Lord, and make an atonement for it; and shall take of the blood of the bullock, and of the blood of the goat, and put it upon the horns of the altar round about.

The testing of works and gift presentations are now over. The court and Tent of Meeting can now house all of God's people coming from the four corners of the earth.

16:19 And he shall sprinkle of the blood upon it with his finger seven times, and cleanse it, and hallow it from the uncleanness of the children of Israel.

The sacrificing of Christ and His church is over. This is the third seven, representing total spiritual perfection and purifying. Does the sprinkling of the altar seven times refer to the earth being purified by

Tabernacle Gifts

God's wrath, represented by the seven trumpets of Revelation 8?[liii]

16:20 And when he hath made an end of reconciling the holy place, and the tabernacle of the congregation, and the altar, he shall bring the live goat:

Now He will rid God's house of the lack of gifts.

16:21 And Aaron shall lay both his hands upon the head of the live goat, and confess over him all the iniquities of the children of Israel, and all their transgressions in all their sins, putting them upon the head of the goat, and shall send him away by the hand of a fit man into the wilderness:

The lack of gifts (think of an empty bowl) will be handed back to these non-sacrificial Christians. They will be asked to throw out the empty bowl (walk out the scapegoat) into an empty place. These Christians will have missed the greatest opportunity of their earthly lives, the privilege to serve Christ. How useless to not have used a sprinkled heart to produce gifts for God.[xcviii] However, they are saved.

All Christians are designated by God to be assistant priests. However, Christians have a choice to *act* like assistant priests[lxxxiii] on earth or to ignore their priestly duties and *act* like non-priests.[lxxxix]

Appendix A

Each animal brought into the court was a sin offering and most probably had sin placed on it through confession along with the high priest laying his hands on it. The placing of sin on the scapegoat was more pronounced because of the lack of a resulting sacrifice. This was to stress the shamefulness of not using a sprinkled heart for God.[xcvii]

16:22 And the goat shall bear upon him all their iniquities unto a land not inhabited: and he shall let go the goat in the wilderness.

The lack of gifts is removed and sent to an empty place. The scripture says the "goat shall bear" because the goat was not sacrificed. Another way of saying this is, "After confessing sin on this goat, it will not be sacrificed." Especially important is that there was no blood from this goat, blood needs to be shed and properly used (sprinkled) for this goat to be of any benefit (Heb. 9:22).

16:23 And Aaron shall come into the tabernacle of the congregation, and shall put off the linen garments, which he put on when he went into the holy place, and shall leave them there:

Christ is fully revealed as God in all His Glory.

16:24 And he shall wash his flesh with water in the holy place, and put on his garments, and come forth, and offer his burnt offering, and the

Tabernacle Gifts

burnt offering of the people, and make an atonement for himself, and for the people.

Once all New Testament Christians arrive in heaven and have all been tested, Jesus, revealed in all His Divine Glory, will offer both results of His work to God: both New and Old Testament saints represented by burning the entire part of both rams, showing that no saint will be left out. What a celebration this event will be in heaven.

16:25 And the fat of the sin offering shall he burn upon the altar.

"The fat of the sin offering": He will rejoice that all this work is done and all His people are now with Him.

16:26 And he that let go the goat for the scapegoat shall wash his clothes, and bathe his flesh in water, and afterward come into the camp.

Non-sacrificial Christians do not sacrifice on earth. The full bath (Rom. 6:3–4) indicates a scene change in this prophecy from heaven to earth, a change in nature from a spiritual scene back to a mortal scene.

16:27 And the bullock for the sin offering, and the goat for the sin offering, whose blood was brought in to make atonement in the holy place, shall one carry forth without the camp; and they

Appendix A

shall burn in the fire their skins, and their flesh, and their dung.

Jesus sacrificed on the earth and was rejected by the ungodly. We are to follow His example.

16:28 And he that burneth them shall wash his clothes, and bathe his flesh in water, and afterward he shall come into the camp.

Sacrificial Christians sacrifice on earth by following Christ's example. They are also rejected by godless men as Christ was.

16:29–31 And this shall be a statute for ever unto you: that in the seventh month, on the tenth day of the month, ye shall afflict your souls, and do no work at all, whether it be one of your own country, or a stranger that sojourneth among you: For on that day shall the priest make an atonement for you, to cleanse you, that ye may be clean from all your sins before the Lord. It shall be a sabbath of rest unto you, and ye shall afflict your souls, by a statute for ever.

Truly this is the Highest Holy day of the year, a time when all labors will be put to an end and we all will enter into the true rest. Spiritual perfection (seventh month) will be totally complete (tenth day).

That is the reason the Day of Atonement is celebrated in the 7th month of the Hebrew calendar.

Tabernacle Gifts

Jesus died and was resurrected at Passover in the 1st month. Forty days later, Jesus entered heaven to *start* the Day of Atonement ceremony. Christians of this time (7th time-segment) will *finish* the ceremony with our arrival and gift-giving, when the trump of God is heard!

16:32–34 And the priest, whom he shall anoint, and whom he shall consecrate to minister in the priest's office in his father's stead, shall make the atonement, and shall put on the linen clothes, even the holy garments: And he shall make an atonement for the holy sanctuary, and he shall make an atonement for the tabernacle of the congregation, and for the altar, and he shall make an atonement for the priests, and for all the people of the congregation. And this shall be an everlasting statute unto you, to make an atonement for the children of Israel for all their sins once a year. And he did as the LORD commanded Moses.

The description of the day is repeated to stress its immense importance. The Holy Spirit is saying that the true High Priest, who is anointed and appointed by God the Father, who comes as God's Son and by God's oath, will come as a man and make atonement for all men and mediate a new covenant with God on their behalf. This atonement will be done once on the true Day of Atonement.

Appendix B

∽ Traditional Interpretations ∼ & FAQs

The following is an attempt to reconcile the foregoing with traditional interpretations of the goats' meanings and also to answer some FAQs.

The sacrificial goat could represent Jesus' work. Accepting Jesus' sacrifice allows Him to work in us. Therefore it could be said that the sacrificial goat represents the work of Christ in us.

for it is God who works in you to will and to act according to his good purpose. (Phil. 2:13 NIV)

The scapegoat could represent wickedness sent into the wilderness. If a person claims to be a Christian and does not have deeds or work, can such faith save him?

Tabernacle Gifts

What doth it profit, my brethren, though a man say he hath faith, and have not works? can faith save him? If a brother or sister be naked, and destitute of daily food, And one of you say unto them, Depart in peace, be ye warmed and filled; notwithstanding ye give them not those things which are needful to the body; what doth it profit? Even so faith, if it hath not works, is dead, being alone. Yea, a man may say, Thou hast faith, and I have works: shew me thy faith without thy works, and I will shew thee my faith by my works. Thou believest that there is one God; thou doest well: the devils also believe, and tremble. But wilt thou know, O vain man, that faith without works is dead? Was not Abraham our father justified by works, when he had offered Isaac his son upon the altar? Seest thou how faith wrought with his works, and by works was faith made perfect? And the scripture was fulfilled which saith, Abraham believed God, and it was imputed unto him for righteousness: and he was called the Friend of God. Ye see then how that by works a man is justified, and not by faith only. Likewise also was not Rahab the harlot justified by works, when she had received the messengers, and had sent them out another way? For as the body without the spirit is dead, so faith without works is dead also. (James 2:14–26 KJV)

Appendix B

Frequently Asked Question: Number One

What about the fact that the Day of Atonement offerings appear only to be for sin? Can we be a part of a sin offering?

Jesus' work completely atoned for our sin; we have no part in that. However, Christians need to do their part to complete the work Jesus started. We, in effect, fill in after Him our part (sacrificial life) of His work, for His church, which is our priestly duty (Rom. 15:16).

Now I rejoice in what was suffered for you, and I fill up in my flesh what is still lacking in regard to Christ's afflictions, for the sake of his body, which is the church. (Col. 1:24 NIV)

In addition, it is important to notice that in Leviticus 16, the people represent people and the animals represent the efforts/results of those people.

Tabernacle Gifts

Frequently Asked Question: Number Two

What about Leviticus 16:21 and 22; it seems these verses have the high priest putting sin on the scapegoat. What does this mean?

Hebrews 13:11 states that the bull and goat sacrifices are sin offerings. Hence, all three animals had sin placed on them: two through sacrifice, one through prayer. A sin offering always required that the priest put his hands[liv] on the animal and confess[lv] sins prior to sacrificing it. In Leviticus 16, this was most probably done with the bull and sacrificial goat. The placing of sin on the scapegoat is more pronounced because there was no resulting sacrifice. This was to stress the shamefulness of not using a sprinkled heart for God.[xcvii]

In Leviticus 16:5, the true High Priest, Jesus, shall take from the world all who belong to Him. As examined earlier, many will have sacrificial gifts for God the Father; however, many will not have gifts after the fire tests them. The lack of gifts is shameful to Christ. His sacrifice sprinkled *all* believers' hearts with His blood. All believers were supposed to bring God gifts. It is impossible for them to have a second chance; earthly life is over. They cannot again crucify for themselves the Son of God to start the process over. Normally, when the high priest put his hand on

Appendix B

an animal and confessed sin, that animal was slaughtered and sacrificed. In the case of the scapegoat, it was let go, which was a shameful thing; sin was covered, but a sacrifice did not occur. Some Bible commentators assume that this goat died in the wilderness. However, the Bible makes no mention of the scapegoat's blood and without sprinkled blood even if this goat died it would be of no benefit as stated in Hebrews 9:22. Christ's sacrifice covered the hearts of these believers, sprinkled hearts that did *not* produce gifts for God. The scapegoat represents the absence of gifts from a blood-covered heart.[xcviii]

For it is impossible for those who were once enlightened, and have tasted of the heavenly gift, and were made partakers of the Holy Ghost, And have tasted the good word of God, and the powers of the world to come, If they shall fall away, to renew them again unto repentance; seeing they crucify to themselves the Son of God afresh, and put him to an open shame. (Heb. 6:4–6 KJV)

The next two verses contrast the good work of the sacrificial Christian and the lack of good work on the part of the scapegoat Christian. The first describes the sacrificial Christian, who is compared to a field. After the field receives rain, that field yields a good crop for the person who owns and cultivates the field, God. After yielding this crop, that field receives a blessing from God.

Tabernacle Gifts

For the earth which drinketh in the rain that cometh oft upon it, and bringeth forth herbs meet for them by whom it is dressed, receiveth blessing from God: (Heb. 6:7 KJV)

The scapegoat (lazy) Christian is also compared to a field. However, after this field receives rain, the crop is worthless or non-existent. The worthless crop is burned and thrown out. The field, representative of the person, is *close* to being cursed by God, but is not cursed.

But that which beareth thorns and briers is rejected, and is nigh unto cursing; whose end is to be burned. (Heb. 6:8 KJV)

Appendix B

Frequently Asked Question: Number Three

We have heard that the scapegoat represented our sins being removed from us, "as far as the east is from the west."(Ps.103:12). Is this false?

As far as the east is from the west, So far has He removed our transgressions from us. (Ps. 103:12 NASB)

This scripture was written by David while under the old covenant that God had with the children of Israel. The children of Israel are referred to earlier in the psalm.

The LORD performs righteous deeds And judgments for all who are oppressed. He made known His ways to Moses, His acts to the sons of Israel. (Ps. 103:6–7 NASB)

The writer of Hebrews (the apostle Paul) tells us that has all changed. Paul states that the old covenant was made obsolete and replaced with a new one. No longer do our sins regularly need to be removed from us by sacrifices. Now, by one sacrifice, our sins are permanently *forgotten*.

Tabernacle Gifts

"BEHOLD, DAYS ARE COMING, SAYS THE LORD, WHEN I WILL EFFECT A NEW COVENANT WITH THE HOUSE OF ISRAEL AND WITH THE HOUSE OF JUDAH; NOT LIKE THE COVENANT WHICH I MADE WITH THEIR FATHERS ON THE DAY WHEN I TOOK THEM BY THE HAND TO LEAD THEM OUT OF THE LAND OF EGYPT; FOR THEY DID NOT CONTINUE IN MY COVENANT, AND I DID NOT CARE FOR THEM, SAYS THE LORD. (Heb. 8:8–9 NASB)

"FOR I WILL BE MERCIFUL TO THEIR INIQUITIES, AND I WILL REMEMBER THEIR SINS NO MORE." **When He said, "A new covenant," He has made the first obsolete. But whatever is becoming obsolete and growing old is ready to disappear. (Heb. 8:12–13 NASB)**

David had much to thank God for, because God provided through the old covenant a way for his sins to be regularly purified (removed) through animal sacrifice. But we have much more to rejoice about, because Jesus provides a way through the new covenant for our sins to be forgotten and never to require removal again! Yes, Jesus removed our sins from us one time through His death on the cross; however, Hebrews 13:11–13 makes reference to the dead carcasses as showing this, not the live scapegoat. Our sins were paid for (removed) by Jesus' death on the cross, not a live walk in the desert.

For by one offering He has perfected for all time those who are sanctified. And the Holy Spirit

Appendix B

also testifies to us; for after saying, "THIS IS THE COVENANT THAT I WILL MAKE WITH THEM AFTER THOSE DAYS, SAYS THE LORD: I WILL PUT MY LAWS UPON THEIR HEART, AND ON THEIR MIND I WILL WRITE THEM," **He then says,** AND THEIR SINS AND THEIR LAWLESS DEEDS I WILL REMEMBER NO MORE." **Now where there is forgiveness of these things, there is no longer any offering for sin. (Heb. 10:14–18 NASB)**

For Christians, sin has been permanently removed through Jesus' one-time sacrifice, not the lack of sacrifice, and permanently forgotten by God the Father, not just walked far into the west.

Since Psalm 103:12 deals with sins being removed, doesn't this psalm also have a new covenant meaning? To answer that question, let's look at this verse in its full context, by including verse 11, which is rarely quoted.

For as high as the heavens are above the earth, So great is His lovingkindness toward those who fear Him. As far as the east is from the west, So far has He removed our transgressions from us. (Ps. 103:11–12 NASB)

All sin comes from rebellion against God. What this psalm is saying in verse 11 is that God sent His Son from heaven to earth (His love is as high as the heavens are above the earth). God loved us so much that he sent Jesus (His love) from heaven to earth

Tabernacle Gifts

(from high to low) to redeem those who fear Him (choose to obey). In verse 12, His Son removed our rebellion against God. It is not that sin will be placed east or west (sin is forgotten, not placed), but that we as Christians will now follow Christ in a different direction, the direction of obedience, away from rebellion. Christians follow Jesus a new direction toward heaven and away from rebellion, through *repentance*, which is the act of changing our direction. The key words in verse 12: east, west, and transgressions reveal this true meaning when the Hebrew words are studied. East and west should actually be translated as eastward or westward, and transgressions should be translated as rebellion.

The sacrificial bull followed by the sacrificial goat on the Day of Atonement, in both sacrifice and in being burned outside the camp, demonstrated both verses of Psalm 103. The sacrificial bull demonstrated God's love, and the sacrificial goat demonstrated a Christian's repentance.[29]

Couldn't all these concepts be demonstrated in the scapegoat? One-time removal because it was walked out, forgotten sin (or rebellion) because it was put as far as the east is from the west, and a new direction because it was sent into the wilderness? Let's take each question separately. First, how are sins removed from us? Sin is removed by Jesus' work on the cross at Calvary. His death removed the penalty

---

[29]*In Leviticus 16, the people represent people and the animals represent the efforts/results of those people.*

Appendix B

of sin. Therefore, the scapegoat could not represent removal because the scapegoat was not sacrificed, unlike Jesus, who was sacrificed. It was the dead bull's carcass that represented removal on the Day of Atonement.

Second, how are sins separated from us (east from west)? Separation occurs each time a sinner confesses his or her sins; God then remembers them no more. Therefore, the scapegoat could not represent separation because the goat is left alive[30] in the wilderness where it could possibly be found. In which case, it is something that could be remembered; hence the scapegoat could not represent permanent separation. Separation was represented on the Day of Atonement when the high priest laid his hands on each animal and confessed sin. All three sin offering animals had sin confessed; all three were taken outside the camp: two were carried and one was walked. At that point all sins were forgotten.

However, confession is just the first step of sin's separation; the second step is to *repent*, which is to truly walk away from rebellion (or sin) and follow Jesus in obedience. This was most clearly demonstrated by the sacrificial goat on the Day of Atonement, not the scapegoat. After the scapegoat had sins confessed, the non-priest Levite took it a different way.

---

[30] The Bible makes no mention of the scapegoat's blood and without **sprinkled** blood even if this goat died it would be of no benefit as stated in Hebrews 9:22.

Frequently Asked Question: Number Four

What about Enoch and Elijah? Didn't they go directly to heaven? Didn't they need Jesus?

Jesus is the only way to God. Even Enoch and Elijah needed to accept Jesus as their Lord and personal Savior to enter heaven. In Genesis 5:24, the Bible states that God took Enoch; however, it does not say where He brought him.

And Enoch walked with God: and he was not; for God took him. (Gen. 5:24 KJV)

In Hebrews, the apostle Paul tells us the rest of the story. He says that Enoch's faith pleased God so much, that God simply spared Enoch the agony of death.

By faith Enoch was taken from this life, so that he did not experience death; he could not be found, because God had taken him away. For before he was taken, he was commended as one who pleased God. (Heb. 11:5–6 NIV)

Neither Genesis nor Hebrews states that Enoch went to heaven, but only that God spared him from

Appendix B

death. Romans 5:14 makes it clear that Enoch was a sinner requiring Jesus just like us. Therefore, we must presume that Enoch went directly to paradise (Abraham's bosom) in Sheol where all the Old Testament righteous went. In fact, all men must die and all saints must be resurrected by Christ as described in 1 Corinthians 15:12–23. First Corinthians 15:7 specifically states that without an actual resurrection faith is futile.

Elijah was one of God's prophets. In the same chapter of Hebrews, Paul mentions that "the prophets" also pleased God by faith.

And what more shall I say? For time will fail me if I tell of Gideon, Barak, Samson, Jephthah, of David and Samuel and the prophets, (Heb. 11:32 NASB)

Finally, at the conclusion of Hebrews 11, after describing the incredible faith of the Old Testament righteous, Paul states that all the people described (which included Enoch and the prophet Elijah) did not receive the promise and were not made perfect, but had to wait and receive it together with us.

And all these, having gained approval through their faith, did not receive what was promised, because God had provided something better for us, so that apart from us they would not be made perfect. (Heb. 11:39–40 NASB)

Tabernacle Gifts

Jesus is the promise, the new covenant, and redemption comes only through Him. That is why even a very good person does not go to heaven without Jesus.

However, let's look a little closer at Elijah. Didn't the Bible specifically say he was taken up to heaven?

As they were walking along and talking together, suddenly a chariot of fire and horses of fire appeared and separated the two of them, and Elijah went up to heaven in a whirlwind. (2 Kings 2:11–12 NIV)

In the Bible, there are three heavens described by Scripture. For example, the apostle Paul went to the third heaven.

I know a man in Christ who fourteen years ago was caught up to the third heaven. Whether it was in the body or out of the body I do not know—God knows. (2 Cor. 12:2 NIV)

The three heavens are: the air, outer space, and the heaven where God is. Most translations of the Bible use the same word to describe each of them. Elijah was simply taken into the air, the first heaven. From there he was most likely taken directly to Abraham in Sheol. The Bible does not say that he was taken to God, in the third heaven. James 5:17 says that Elijah was a man just like us (a sinner). Therefore he would need Jesus before he could go to

Appendix B

the Father. In fact John 14:6 makes it clear: No one can go to the Father without Jesus.

Jesus answered, "I am the way and the truth and the life. No one comes to the Father except through me (John 14:6 NIV)

Tabernacle Gifts

ᐠ Afterword ᐠ

When first looking at the activity in the court on the Day of Atonement, it appeared that the day started with seven primary elements: four primary people (high priest, Levitical priest, non-priest Levite, the camp) and three primary animals (bull, sacrificed goat, scapegoat). Of the animals, two were seen left in the court and one sent out. The one animal sent out had sins placed on it.

But under further examination, it is apparent that all three animals were sent out: two were carried and one was walked. All three animals in effect had sins placed on them: two through sacrifice and one through prayer. As a result, all four people had their sins covered. Now, what remained in the court were two bowls of blood (gifts) and three people, (high priest, Levitical priest and non-priest Levite). Each of the three had their sins covered and were in the *court*, two had representative gifts remaining, and one had nothing.

Lastly, do not let this issue of the exact interpretation of the goats hinder your accepting the message of this book. Lawyers often put a clause in contracts that states, "If any part of this contract fails to hold up in court, that part will be removed, but the rest of the contract will stand." Feel free to reject any part of this book that may not hold up to your interpretations; however, keep the good parts!

Appendix C

～ Scipture Citations ～

[i] 1 Kings 8:3–4; 1 Kings 8:6
[ii] Ex. 27:9
[iii] Ex. 38:13–14
[iv] Num. 2:1–2
[v] Num. 3:38
[vi] Ex. 27:1
[vii] Ex. 40:28
[viii] Ex. 25:31–32
[ix] Ex. 26:35
[x] Lev. 24:5–8
[xi] Ex. 30:1–3
[xii] Ex. 26:33
[xiii] Ex. 25:10–11
[xiv] Ex. 25:17–21
[xv] Ex. 25:22
[xvi] Ex. 39:43
[xvii] Ex. 40:34
[xviii] Lev. 24:2
[xix] Ps. 80:1
[xx] Ex. 13:21–22
[xxi] Ex. 40:36–38
[xxii] Ex. 28:1
[xxiii] Num. 4:20
[xxiv] Lev. 16:29–31
[xxv] Lev. 16:34
[xxvi] Lev. 16:14
[xxvii] Lev. 16:8–10
[xxviii] Heb. 7:12–14
[xxix] Rom. 10:9
[xxx] Rev. 1:20
[xxxi] 1 Peter 3:18; Acts 1:9
[xxxii] Matt. 27:51
[xxxiii] Rev. 19:8
[xxxiv] 1 John 1:9
[xxxv] Hag. 2:6–9
[xxxvi] Rom. 6:4
[xxxvii] Rev. 20:6
[xxxviii] Heb. 9:6–8
[xxxix] Rom. 14:10
[xl] Lev. 16:15

Tabernacle Gifts

xli Ps. 100:4
xlii Acts 2:22
xliii James 2:15–16
xliv Isa. 53:2–3; Ex, 38:8
xlv James 1:9–11
xlvi Ps. 66:1–20
xlvii Rev. 12:4
xlviii Dan. 10:11
xlix Gen. 3:24
l Gen. 9:13
li Rev. 12:7–9
lii Acts 12:15
liii Rev. 8:1–6
liv Lev. 8:14
lv Lev. 5:5–6
lvi Rom. 6:23
lvii John 1:14
lviii Phil. 2:6–8
lix Rom. 1:4
lx Jere. 31:31–34
lxi Heb. 3:1; 1 Cor. 9:24–27; Rom. 15:16; Heb. 12:18,22; Heb.13:10
lxii Phil. 3:12–15; 1 Peter 1:13–16
lxiii Luke 8:17
lxiv Heb. 9:11
lxv Heb. 8:2-5
lxvi Luke 24:31
lxvii Isa. 63:3
lxviii Heb. 13:10
lxix Rom. 11:13–21; Rev. 2:5
lxx Isa. 44:22–23; Heb. 10:20
lxxi Micah 2:12–13; Ps. 24:7–10
lxxii Acts 4:12; John 14:6; Col.1:18
lxxiii Heb. 9:19, 23
lxxiv Rev. 5:7
lxxv 2 Sam. 6:2
lxxvi Heb. 9:18,23
lxxvii Rev. 5:8; Rev. 8:3
lxxviii Heb. 3:16–19
lxxix 1 John 5:6
lxxx 2 Cor. 2:16
lxxxi Heb. 8:3; Rev. 5
lxxxii Phil. 2:5; John 13:15–17
lxxxiii 2 Cor. 2:14–16
lxxxiv Acts 1:26
lxxxv Heb. 6:12
lxxxvi Heb. 12:4
lxxxvii Rev. 3:19; Heb. 12:5–13; Acts 15:36–40
lxxxviii Rom. 15:16; 2 Cor. 3:6; 2 Cor. 5:9; Phil. 3:17; 2 Tim. 2:1–7; 1 Peter 1: 13–16; Luke 12:36–38; Phil. 3:16; 1 Peter chpts. 1–5; Isa. 66:21; Acts 4:36–37
lxxxix 1 Tim. 6:9–10; 2 Tim. 2:16-18; 2 Tim. 4:9-10,16; 1 Peter 2:1–3; 1 John 2:11; Luke 12: 47–48; Heb. 12:1; Luke 10:30–37; Acts 5:1–10; 2 Thes. 3:6–15; 1 Cor. 5:12; Gal. 6:1; Luke 14:34–35; 1 Peter chpts. 1–5; Isa. 66:21
xc Heb. 2:10
xci John 10:3; Num. 3:38
xcii Rom. 10:12
xciii John 10:4
xciv Heb. 11:13–16
xcv Rev. 3:5
xcvi Rom. 6:3–4
xcvii 2 Tim. 2:15; Heb. 6:12; 1 Thes. 4:1–8
xcviii 2 Cor. 3:3
xcix 1 Peter 2:21
c Ps. 110

Bibliography

The Wycliffe Bible Commentary, electronic database (Chicago: Moody, 1962).

Vine's Expository Dictionary of Biblical Words (Nashville: Thomas Nelson, 1985).

The New Unger's Bible Dictionary (Chicago: Moody, 1966).

Treasury of Scripture Knowledge, electronic database (Seattle: Biblesoft, 1993).

PC Study Bible's Greek-Hebrew Dictionary and Englishman's Concordance Simplified Transliteration Guide (Galaxie Software, 1992).

Thayer's Greek Lexicon, electronic database (Seattle: Biblesoft, 2000).

Nelson's Illustrated Bible Dictionary (Nashville: Thomas Nelson, 1986).

Nave's Topical Bible, electronic database (Seattle: Biblesoft and TriStar, 1990).

Tabernacle Gifts

Matthew Henry's Commentary on the Whole Bible, New Modern Edition, electronic database (Seattle: Hendrickson, 1991).

International Standard Bible Encyclopedia, electronic database (Seattle: Biblesoft, 1995–96).

Biblesoft's New Exhaustive Strong's Numbers and Concordance with Expanded Greek-Hebrew Dictionary (Seattle: Biblesoft and International Bible Translators, 1994).

Interlinear Transliterated Bible (Seattle: Biblesoft, 1994).

Fausset's Bible Dictionary, electronic database (Seattle: Biblesoft, 1998).

Barne's Notes, electronic database (Seattle: Biblesoft, 1997).

Biblesoft PC Study Bible v3.1 for Windows (Seattle: Biblesoft, 1993–2000).

Kevin J. Conner, *The Tabernacle of Moses* (Seattle: City Bible Publishing, 1976).

M. R. DeHaan MD, *The Tabernacle* (Grand Rapids: Zondervan, 1955).

Ryrie Study Bible (Notes) (Chicago: Moody, 1986, 1995).

Ervin N. Hershberger, *Seeing Christ in the Tabernacle* (Fairfax: Choice Books of Northern Virginia, 1995).

~ Author's Information ~

Undergraduate Purdue University; Graduate DePaul University; Deacon, Parkway Hills Baptist Church, Plano, TX; Married; Father of three; Christian since 1974.

Note from the author regarding the treatment of Scripture block quotations:

"The 'as is' manner in which the Scripture block quotations are recorded is different from generally accepted practice. This has to do with the way in which I study God's Word. I study the Word 'as is' and then search for its meaning. The fact that the references are bold and not indented has to do with the importance of God's Word over my words."

Ordering Information

This book is available as listed below. However, this publication may be purchased by your church, fellowship, or seminary at a quantity discount. Please contact the publisher for a discount schedule. In addition, a 17x 24- color print of the tabernacle artwork is also available for purchase.

CALL toll free 1-877-818-7154 to order using your credit card.

Description	Price	Quantity	Total
ISBN 0-970454-80-5 Tabernacle Gifts—Messianic Edition	$10.95		
ISBN 0-970454-81-3 Tabernacle Gifts—Evangelical Edition	$10.95		
Artwork: 17 x 24 Lithograph Color Print "Moses' Tabernacle in the Wilderness"	$23.95		

Subtotal: _____
Discount if any*: _____
Tax: in Texas add 8.25% (.90/book; 1.98/picture)**: _____
Postage and Handling***: _____
Total: _____

* Ten or more please contact the publisher for the discount schedule.
** If tax-exempt please provide exemption certificate.
***$3.99 for the first book and/or picture and $1.99 for each additional.

OR MAIL order form and make check payable as shown below:

Michael Zarlengo Publishing
17194 Preston Road Suite 123-142, Dallas, Texas 75248
SAN 253-4576